You Can Have IT!

MORE THAN 125 DECADENT DIABETES-FRIENDLY RECIPES

DEVIN ALEXANDER

With a Foreword by Akbar Gbajabiamila

Food Photography by Mittera
Lifestyle Photography by Michelle Pederson

American Diabetes Association.

Associate Publisher, Books, Abe Ogden; Managing Editor, Rebekah Renshaw; Acquisitions Editor, Victor Van Beuren; Editor, Lauren Wilson; Cover Design and Composition, pixiedesign, llc; Food Photographer, Mittera; Lifestyle Photographer, Michelle Pederson; Printer, LSC Communications.

Printed in the United States of America
1 3 5 7 9 10 8 6 4 2

The suggestions and information contained in this publication are generally consistent with the Standards of Medical Care in Diabetes and other policies of the American Diabetes Association, but they do not represent the policy or position of the Association or any of its boards or committees. Reasonable steps have been taken to ensure the accuracy of the information presented. However, the American Diabetes Association cannot ensure the safety or efficacy of any product or service described in this publication. Individuals are advised to consult a physician or other appropriate health care professional before undertaking any diet or exercise program or taking any medication referred to in this publication. Professionals must use and apply their own professional judgment, experience, and training and should not rely solely on the information contained in this publication before prescribing any diet, exercise, or medication. The American Diabetes Association—its officers, directors, employees, volunteers, and members—assumes no responsibility or liability for personal or other injury, loss, or damage that may result from the suggestions or information in this publication.

The American Diabetes Association cannot ensure the safety or efficacy of any product, technique, or service described on www.devinalexander.com/diabetes. Brand name recommendations have not been endorsed by the American Diabetes Association, and the American Diabetes Association assumes no responsibility or liability for the suggestions or information on this website.

Madelyn Wheeler conducted the internal review of this book to ensure that it meets American Diabetes Association guidelines.

∞ The paper in this publication meets the requirements of the ANSI Standard Z39.48-1992 (permanence of paper).

ADA titles may be purchased for business or promotional use or for special sales. To purchase more than 50 copies of this book at a discount, or for custom editions of this book with your logo, contact the American Diabetes Association at the address below or at booksales@diabetes.org.

American Diabetes Association
2451 Crystal Drive, Suite 900
Arlington, VA 22202

Library of Congress Cataloging-in-Publication Data

   Names: Alexander, Devin, author. | American Diabetes Association.
   Title: You can have it : more than 125 decadent diabetes-friendly recipes /
      Devin Alexander.
   Description: Arlington : American Diabetes Association, [2018] | Includes
      index.
   Identifiers: LCCN 2017016618 | ISBN 9781580406833
   Subjects: LCSH: Diabetes--Diet therapy--Recipes. | Diabetes--Nutritional
      aspects. | LCGFT: Cookbooks.
   Classification: LCC RC662 .A39 2018 | DDC 641.5/6314--dc23
   LC record available at https://lccn.loc.gov/2017016618

THIS BOOK IS DEDICATED TO
Trevor Benjamin Simone and Quinn Simone-Thornton,
my adorable, superhero nephews, who've brought
so much joy and even renewed health to my family...
in hopes that your generation reverses preventable
chronic illness while enjoying every bite you consume!

Want a little extra help with the recipes in this book?

Visit **www.devinalexander.com/diabetes**

f facebook.com/devinalexander

🐦 @ChefDevin

📷 devinalexander

▶ chefdevinalexander

in devinalexander

Table of Contents

Foreword

by Akbar Gbajabiamila

EATING HEALTHY IS A CHOICE. It's an active, conscious choice to want to do what's best for your body, every day. People always tell me how challenging it is for them to eat healthy, or go into detail about all the reasons why they are not choosing a better lifestyle for themselves. Trust me, I understand the challenges, but unhealthy eating is also a choice, one that will negatively impact your body for a long time.

I played five seasons in the NFL before making the transition to TV as the host of NBC's *American Ninja Warrior* and the NFL Network's *Fantasy Live*. I'm 6'6", 250 pounds, a father of four beautiful children, husband to my incredible wife, and a food addict.

Playing in the league in my twenties, I could basically eat anything I wanted. I burned upward of 10,000 calories a day, so food was truly my friend. Now that I'm 38 and retired, I had to find a way to still get the food I loved while making healthy choices for myself and setting a good example for my family. The notion of "pay for it now" or "pay for it later" when it comes to health consistently rings in my mind. It is far too easy to fall into the "fix it" trap once a problem does arise, rather than making proactive conscious choices prior to an issue coming up.

As a society, we are very detached from not only where our food is coming from but what we're putting in our mouths and feeding our families. Growing up in Los Angeles, I saw firsthand the effects of unhealthy diets. I understand how hard it is to get affordable yet healthy and delicious food. But I also know how deadly and life threating the other options can be. I watched one of my closest friends develop diabetes as a young man due to his poor diet. I watched other friends live on junk food because their parents made the easy and affordable choice of fast food restaurants.

As a father, it is extremely important to me that I set my children up for a lifetime of health and wellness, and I know that starts with their food choices. Sometimes though, this isn't always realistic. For a family on the go, always balancing the speed of life, healthy food choices frequently become the first thing to go.

In this mighty cookbook by Devin Alexander, she helps to create a solution for this ongoing struggle. She proves that you can eat well, while also making meals easy, delicious, and family friendly! Forget about the days of living on celery and carrots to feel "healthy". What's that old saying? You can have your cake and eat it too? That's right; Devin shows us how to cook tasty, low glucose treats, meals, and everything in between! She truly gives "delicious" a whole new meaning! This book is jam packed with tasty, easy, AND healthy recipes that your whole family will love.

Whether this is the first healthy cookbook you've picked up or you're looking to make a lifestyle change, always remember, you have one body, one opportunity, one moment, one today—so make the active choice to take control of your life and your food intake for a better, brighter tomorrow!

Preface

THEY SAY CATS HAVE 9 LIVES. Well, when this cookbook goes to print, I'll have 9 books...and I'm hoping this 9th book actually *saves* lives!

At 15 years old, I weighed 200 pounds and was on the fast track for many diseases. My pediatrician, Dr. Carabello, made that very clear. Imagine my horror as I listened to him tell my mother what I should eat! I hated most vegetables—and pretty much anything that was good for me. Plain chicken and boiled eggs weren't happening, and my parents' whispers of sending me to "fat camp," as the kids at school called it, horrified me! I was bullied for my weight every day at school, and I was a plus size model, so I was constantly told, "You have such a pretty face". While that may sound like a compliment, what I heard and felt at the time was, "What a waste..." As much as I knew I wanted to change and live a healthier lifestyle, I believed it would take a great deal of willpower. I've never had willpower. To this day, I still have no willpower.

To add insult to injury, my Italian grandmother, who was a phenomenal cook, was my number one role model. Unlike me, she was a classic beauty. In fact, she was in the Miss America Pageant, was Miss Greater Philadelphia, and her list of crowns goes on. I did, however, inherit her cooking skills. A blessing? At the time I didn't think so. But overweight and bullied or not, I was not giving up my Italian heritage or my deep love for food. Plus, cooking was the only thing I was good at. So I was stuck...or was I?

It was actually cooking that saved my life! And I've now dedicated my more than 20 year career (so far) to cooking in the hopes that others who are as stuck as I felt at 15 years old and who love food as much as I do always have real food options. Real options that allow them to invite friends over for dinner without anyone ever knowing they're serving healthy food. Real options for an insanely happy life!

When I was 15 years old, if you took all 15-year-olds and measured their fitness, I would likely have fallen in the least healthy one percentile of my peers. And I felt unattractive. Now, at 45 years old (as I write this), I'm likely in the 1% most healthy among 45-year-olds—and NOT because I'm more disciplined or better at living a healthy lifestyle than anyone else! It's because I have the ability and obsessive desire to spend too much time in my kitchen—and this time has paid off! I've cracked the code for myself (and hopefully, and more importantly, for you too!) on how to make decadent recipes that are actually approved by doctors, dietitians, and now the American Diabetes Association! These recipes are not the "diet food" I tried to eat when I first knew I needed to make a lifestyle change. These are recipes that I actually look forward to making and eating! And I know you will too!

So here's to pizza, burgers, and rich chocolate pudding—and to helping those who have diabetes live richer, fuller, more delicious lives!

Acknowledgments

TO THE AMAZING TEAM WHO ASSISTED ME IN TURNING THIS BOOK FROM A VISION INTO A REALITY: Michelle Pederson, Amy Gassner, Sarah Kasravi, Tricia Takasugi, Emily Scharmann, Barbara Waibing Li, Susan Vandlandingham, Anthony Rizzuto, Maria Solis, Tiffany Shu, Lauren Crittenden, Joseph Teplicky, Audrey Sweetwood, Kathryn Holm, Kimberly Eberhardt, Sandy Levin, and my mother, Toni Simone. Mom, I cherish the time we got to spend together while creating this book. Michelle, you're talented beyond words, and I'm so grateful for all you've contributed to my life for the past 4 years! Amy and L.G., your support has meant the world!

To my entire Biggest Loser Family for embracing my work. And to the former contestants, particularly those who let me into their lives enough to inspire this book: Jennifer Jacobs, Jay Jacobs, Mark Pinhasovich, Olivia Ward, Hannah Curlee Young, Courtney Crozier Respess (& Alex!), "Momma Gail" Lindsay Lee, Marci Crozier, Joe Ostaszewski, Rasha Pecoraro, Mike Messina, Coleen Skeabeck, Ali Vincent, Amanda Arlauskus, Elizabeth Liliana Hanapole, Jennifer Rumple, Aaron Semmel, Gary Deckman, Jim and Bill Germanakos, Amy Cremen, and Shellay Gannaway Cremen.

To Melissa's Produce for supplying the most amazing fruits and veggies to assist in the development of this book—with a special thanks to Robert Schueller for personally delivering it!

To Preya Patel Bhakta for the Elli Quark shipments! And to Sara Wing and the team at Cabot Creamery for always supplying your amazing 75% less fat, extra light sharp cheddar!

To Mike Brophy and Sony VAIO for the awesome tablet.

To A.J. Aumock, Grete Krohn Lavrenz, Annie Dubski, Craig Blakaitis, Atalanta Rafferty, Cassie D'Kae, and the whole team at Truvia!

To the friends who add so much to my life daily: Pam Dzierzanowski, Ben and Suz Graham, Chris Neilsen, Jordan Harris Bracamonte, Amy Williams, Pamela Salzman, Karen Kripilani, Jennifer Proctor, Elaine Metaxas, Angela Mader, Mark Daley, Ashita Johnson, Lisa Coppedge, Tammi Leader Fuller, Timothy Koerner, April Beyer, and "Funny Steve" Swartz. And to Tara Hackley for being the most amazing and fun USTA captain and for letting me burn calories on the best team ever!

To Donny and Ginger Young and the whole beach tennis crew—I truly don't know what I would do without you!

To David Shteif for reminding me exactly what I want and for being there to selflessly help me execute exactly that.

To Christine Lu, Audrey Cavenecia, and Michael Loeb for the Founders and Funders Retreat and for "setting the wheels in motion". And Alicia Dunhams, Wei Huong, and Debra Faris for being amazing connectors!

To my friends and colleagues of the Entrepreneurs Organization, especially Kalika Joy Nacion Yap, Gene Lim, Eddie Espinosa, and Mitch and Paula Langstein for your many contributions to my business—and my happiness!

To Akbar Gbajabiamila for generously writing the foreword to this book. And for Alexy Posner and Scott Manthorne for getting us connected!

To Larry Broughton for putting a smile on my face and lending your taste buds during the last couple of months of writing, even when counting every grain of salt might otherwise have been a bit more frustrating.

To my family for always supporting and encouraging my dreams...even when they make little sense to you.

Finally to Maria Solis, I truly don't know what I would have done without your friendship in recent years, but especially this year. You are one of a kind!

Introduction

This Book is NOT Just for Those Living with Diabetes!

While this book was created by me and the American Diabetes Association following the nutritional guidelines currently recommended by the Association, I have been and truly will continue eating and entertaining with many of the recipes found within these pages. They are not "diet" recipes, or "diabetes recipes". They are high flavor recipes that have been carefully constructed to allow all people, including those with diabetes, to live full, rich, fit lives!

I'm Not Crazy, Just Dedicated

Okay, maybe I'm a little crazy...but that's what allows me to write recipes that always surprise people. As you go deep into this book, you might be surprised by what you find. At first glance, you're definitely going to see gorgeous photos and alluring recipe titles that might have you saying, "There's no way I can eat that!" But as you start to read the recipes, you'll see how precisely the "formulas" have been calculated to make these recipes as healthy as they are delicious. My friends were accusing me of actually counting grains of salt—and they weren't too far off! So, yes, there are measurements in this book like 1/64 teaspoon of salt that you likely won't find in many (if any) other cookbooks. This kind of precision might seem insane. But please keep an open mind and give these recipes a try. The TLC that I put into the recipes on my end to meet the American Diabetes Association's nutritional guidelines is what makes these recipes different than others you're likely to find in a strictly regulated health cookbook. The details in my recipes will take all of the stress away from you (after you hunt down some tiny measuring spoons). I have dedicated an area of my personal website to providing everything you need to know to master these recipes: visit **www.devinalexander.com/diabetes**.[1]

[1] The American Diabetes Association cannot ensure the safety or efficacy of any product, technique, or service described on this website. Brand name recommendations have not been endorsed by the American Diabetes Association, and the American Diabetes Association assumes no responsibility or liability for the suggestions or information on this website.

Forget about Grandma's Rules!

I love my grandmother and I will smile whenever I think of her until the day I die. But you know all those lessons that grandma taught you in the kitchen? Things like: "When you put a toothpick in the center of a baked good, it should come out dry" or "Pork should be cooked until it has no pink left in it at all"? Those "rules" can actually sabotage your healthy kitchen. You'll need to adjust your thinking and forget some of these rules when cooking healthy recipes.

Take the pork rule, for example: yes, you want to make sure your meat is cooked to appropriate and safe temperatures (to that end, I *strongly* suggest buying a meat thermometer and learning how to use it properly), but you also don't want to overcook it. I never eat dry meat. Ever. And I choose the leanest cuts of meat most of the time—I just know how to cook them properly. And this is not because I went to some fancy culinary school. (My culinary teacher actually didn't take me seriously at first, knowing I wanted to cook healthy food. Back in the early 90s, you weren't considered a real chef if you even mentioned the word "health"). I can teach you simple techniques to keep even the leanest cuts of meat moist and tender. Visit **www.devinalexander.com/diabetes** if you'd like me to show you how to make sure your meat is safe to eat, but not dry.

Baking in a healthy kitchen has some different rules as well. For example, because there is no oil in lower fat baked goods to "grease" the toothpick, it won't come out clean when the food is done cooking. Instead it will come out "sticky". So it's important to closely follow the recipes in this book instead of relying on old tricks to tell when a food is done.

The Few Kitchen "Rules" No One Follows That I Really Wish You Would Follow!

While grandma's cooking rules may not always apply to healthier recipes, there are several kitchen rules that will be helpful as you begin your journey through this cookbook:

1. Prep all of your ingredients before you begin cooking. If you don't prepare, you might burn one step trying to prep the next one.

2. Understand that cooking times are guidelines, and all ovens vary. There is no way to put the absolute correct time on a recipe when some people are using gas ovens and stovetops and others are using electric. Use the descriptors given in the recipes as the real indicators of doneness— the numbers are just a guide.

3. Always wash and *dry* all of your produce and herbs. If you don't dry your salad greens, you're guaranteed a soggy salad! And if you don't dry your herbs, they will stick together. This means that when a recipe calls for 1/4 cup of an herb, you'll use way more than you're supposed to because

the wet herb will be compact, not fluffy as dry herbs would be! This seriously throws measurements way off.

4. If food tastes bland and you've had your dried spices for more than 1 year, consider buying new ones. They lose potency over time.

5. Always fresh squeeze limes and lemons and freshly mince your garlic. You can taste the difference when you use fresh ingredients. Buying these items already prepared can ruin an otherwise perfectly great recipe.

6. Read the nutrition label on a package before you buy a food item for the first time. Some items appear the same, but one brand may have 20 mg of sodium and another brand can have a couple hundred mg.

7. You might notice that I often say to heat your pan then spray it with olive oil spray. The idea being that if you spray a pan then heat it, you're just cooking the spray onto the pan. Not only does it make the pan gummy and ruin the nonstick surface, but your oil can burn, giving a bitter flavor to your dish. Several of my recipes will have you spray olive oil directly onto your food, so it's important to use an olive oil spray without propellants. Most of the prefilled olive oil sprays in cans at the grocery store contain propellants and other ingredients so they warn that you cannot spray them directly onto your food. Visit **www.devinalexander.com/diabetes** where I provide suggestions for propellant free cooking spray and so much more.

Tools of the Trade

I could mention here that you really don't need a lot of fancy equipment to be a great home cook (you mostly just need a great chef knife and a couple of good quality nonstick pans). Or I could list a handful of kitchen essentials followed by a collection of other tools that will save you time and/or be fun to use. But as someone who's already authored *New York Times* best sellers, I understand that not many people want to spend a lot of time reading the introductions to cookbooks these days—we do everything online! So I've set up a whole section of my website dedicated to helping you make the most of this cookbook. That section has everything from links to buy the equipment you need (or want) to brand suggestions for some of my favorite foods. So I hope you'll visit me there for the most up to date information and recommendations: **www.devinalexander.com/diabetes**.

Now that's enough introduction. It's time to turn the page to get cooking...and dig in!

Recipe List

BET YOU'RE GONNA LOVE 'EM BREAKFASTS

Easy Ham & Egg Frittata Cups

Bacon & Egg Sweet Potato Breakfast Sandwich

Summer California Breakfast Sandwich

"Fried Egg" Topped Avocado Toast

Roasted Cherry Tomato Topped Goat Cheese Omelet

Scrambled Eggs with Sautéed Shrimp

Weekday Morning Bruschetta Topped Eggs

Bacon, Egg & Cheese Breakfast Salad

Gingerbread Overnight Oats

German Chocolate Overnight Oats

Chocolate Almond Zoats

Chocolate Sweet Cherry Zoats

Happy Tummy Greens Juice

Pineapple Greens Juice

Pumpkin Pie Smoothie

SERVE 'EM UP SANDWICHES, BURGERS & PIZZAS

BBQ Beef Sandwich

Cranberry Aioli Turkey Sandwich

Fat Burner Sandwich

Grilled Chicken Sandwich with Pesto & Roasted Red Pepper

California Cobb Grilled Chicken Sandwich

Curry Chicken Salad Cups

Greek "Gyro" Sandwich

Pesto Margarita Portobello Burger

Drippy Taco Burger

Bánh Mì Burger

Caramelized Sweet Onion Balsamic Burger

Bacon Ranch Flatbread Pizza

Thai Shrimp Flatbread Pizza

Seared Wild Mushroom Toast

PERFECT PARTY FARE & SAVORY SNACKS

Crab Stuffed Shrimp

Salmon Cucumber Party Bites

Waffle Fry BBQ Bites

Party Wontons

Lean & Loaded Nachos

Seasoned Sweet Potato Chips

Snickerdoodle Kettlecorn

Brussels Salmon "Sliders"

Open-Face Bacon Cheese "Sliders"

Shrimp Guac Apps

SIX PACK SALADS

Shrimp, Orange & Avocado Salad

Tuscan Chopped Salad

Spinach Salad with Warm Bacon Dressing

Kale Grapefruit Pomegranate Salad

Asian Brown Rice Salad

Thai Lime Quinoa Salad

Mafia Quinoa Salad

Lemon Pistachio Quinoa Salad

N'Awlins Potato Salad

ENERGIZING ENTRÉES & MAINS

Japanese London Broil

Spice Grilled London Broil

Honey Lime Marinated London Broil

Crockpot Chipotle Steak Simmer

Mom's Favorite Meatloaf

Rosemary Beef Stew

Java London Broil

Herb Butter Rubbed Turkey Breast

Sriracha Mayo Roasted Turkey Breast

Mediterranean Meatballs with Creamy Dill Sauce

Satay Grilled Chicken Breast

Updated Potato Chip
Crusted Chicken

Grilled Harissa Chicken Skewers

Gift Wrapped Mandarin Chicken

Grilled Chicken Zoodle Marinara

Margarita Chicken

Chicken Pinwheels with Sundried
Tomatoes & Goat Cheese

Ranch Slathered Chicken &
Broccoli Stuffed Potato

Chili, Garlic & Basil Chicken Stir-Fry

Chicken Cheesesteak
Lettuce Cups

Pulled Chicken Tacos with
Papaya Slaw

Maple Chili Glazed Pork Tenderloin

Sweet & Spicy Pomegranate
Pork Tenderloin

Grilled Ahi with Olive
Tomato Tapenade

Bacon Confetti Topped Scallops

Wasabi Crusted Salmon

Bruschetta Plank Salmon

Pan Fried Black Cod with Pink
Grapefruit Salsa

Quick Shrimp Tacos

Tomato Feta Shrimp Pasta

Cheesy Lasagna Rollups

Skinny Skampi

SUPERIOR SIDES

Seasoned Curly Fries

Battered Fries

Sea Salt Dusted Crinkle Cuts

Parmesan Garlic Squash "Fries"

Thyme-ly Butternut Squash "Fries"

Rosemary Mashed Potatoes

Chipotle Honey Sweet
Potato Mash

Mediterranean Farro

Roasted Carrots with Creamy
Carrot Top Pesto

Orange Roasted Asparagus

Burst of Lemon Sautéed Spinach

Hot Sesame Spinach

Green Beans with Champagne
Vinaigrette

Dijon Roasted Brussels Sprouts

Sweet Papaya Slaw

Cucumber Jicama Carrot Slaw

Simple Champagne Slaw

Spicy Sriracha Slaw

Watermelon Street "Fries"

DEVINLY DESSERTS & SWEET SIPS

Chocolate Peanut Butter
Wafflewich Sliders

Truer Love in a Bowl

Quick Berry Crumbles à la Mode

Dark Chocolate "Pudding"

Pear "Fries" à la Mode

Apple "Fries" with Creamy
Peanut Butter Dip

Lemon Blueberry Ricotta Tartlets

Watermelon "Cupcakes"

Grilled Peaches with Amaretto
Ricotta & Toasted Almonds

Grilled Pear Boats with Romano,
Walnuts & Black Pepper

Perfect Pumpkin Pie-lets

Strawberry Daiquiri Sorbet

In-The-Clear Root Beer Float

Passionila Cocktail

Sexy Trainer's Strawberry
Caipirinha

Champagne Blackberry Chillers

SLAM DUNK DRESSINGS, SAUCES, DIPS & TOPPINGS

Devinly Whipped Topping

Creamy Peanut Butter Dip

Can-Have Candied Pecans

Garlicky Dill Dip & Sauce

Skinny Dip in a Flash

Creamy Carrot Top Pesto

Renovated Ranch

Rockin' Body Balsamic

Champagne Vinaigrette

Devinly Warm Bacon Dressing

Body Lovin' Bruschetta

Peanut Satay Sauce

THE BASICS DONE RIGHT

Have-On-Hand Grilled Chicken

Quinoa Cooking Instructions

Farro Cooking Instructions

Roasted Garlic

Roasted Red Peppers

WEEKDAY MORNING BRUSCHETTA TOPPED EGGS • 10

Easy Ham & Egg Frittata Cups

One of the first things you learn in culinary school, and something I strongly encourage everyone to do at home, is to pull out and prep all of your ingredients before you start cooking. Not only could this practice alert you if you're out of an ingredient, you also won't find yourself burning chicken because you're trying to chop veggies. That said, this recipe does have one step that I suggest you don't prep in advance; because avocado turns color pretty quickly, it's best to wait until you put the ham and veggies in the egg to cut the avocado. In waiting, you'll be much more likely to serve a restaurant quality breakfast.

Olive oil spray (propellant free)

1 ¼ ounces 98% lean ham steak (preferably nitrate free), cut into small cubes

¼ cup finely chopped red bell pepper

¼ cup finely chopped sweet onion

½ cup 100% liquid egg whites (preferably cage free)

¼ avocado (about 1 ounce), cut into thin slices

Freshly ground black pepper, to taste, if desired

1 Preheat the oven to 350°F. Lightly mist 2 cups of a standard nonstick muffin tin with spray.

2 Place a medium nonstick frying pan over medium heat. Once it's warm, remove the pan from the burner and lightly mist it with spray. Return it to the burner and add the ham, bell pepper, and onion. Cook, stirring them frequently, until the pepper and onion are tender and just starting to brown, about 3–5 minutes. Remove from heat and set aside.

3 Pour the egg whites evenly between the prepared muffin cups, about ¼ cup egg whites in each. Place the muffin tin on top of a baking sheet (the egg may overflow slightly and drip from the frittata cups). Bake them until they are almost set, about 8–10 minutes.

4 Remove from the oven and spoon the ham mixture evenly between the cups (about ¼ cup mixture in each). Continue baking them for 8–12 more minutes, or until the egg is no longer runny. Transfer the muffin tin to a cooling rack and allow the frittatas to sit for 2 minutes.

5 Using a butter knife and a small spatula, carefully lift the frittatas out of the muffin tin and transfer them to a serving plate. Divide the avocado slices evenly between the frittatas. Season them with pepper. Enjoy immediately.

CHOICES/EXCHANGES
2 nonstarchy vegetable, 3 lean protein, 1 fat

PER SERVING
191 calories, 7 g fat, 1 g saturated fat, 0 g trans fat, 30 mg cholesterol, 430 mg sodium, 315 mg potassium, 11 g carbohydrate, 3 g fiber, 2 g sugars, 22 g protein, 20 mg phosphorus

Bacon & Egg Sweet Potato Breakfast Sandwich

In this recipe the sweet potato is swapping in for bread. Some people call this "sweet potato toast," but I like to be realistic—it's really not toast. That being said, it is yummy. It might sound odd at first to swap a sweet potato for bread, but if you think about it, this sandwich is simply an easier, reimagined presentation of the ingredients in a breakfast hash: potato, egg, and bacon! We all know that's a delicious combo! Note that the peel should remain on the potato.

1 ½ slices center cut bacon (preferably nitrate free)

3 large egg whites (preferably cage free)

Freshly ground black pepper, to taste, if desired

2 (¼ inch thick; about 2 ounces each) slices sweet potato, taken from a medium (about 5 ½ × 2 ½ inch) unpeeled sweet potato

Olive oil spray (propellant free)

½ cup arugula leaves, coarse stems removed

Cook's Notes

Look for a sweet potato that isn't too narrow. You want the sweet potato slices to be close to the size of a sandwich or English muffin. And then you want to cut 2 (¼ inch) slices from the center of the potato.

Toaster ovens vary. Watch your sweet potatoes closely the first time you make this recipe so they don't burn.

1 Cut the full slice of bacon in half, so you have 3 equal half slices.

2 In a small bowl, season the egg whites with pepper.

3 Lightly mist both sides of the potato slices with spray. Put them directly on the rack in a toaster oven. Set the toaster oven to the darkest setting, and toast the sweet potatoes as many times as necessary until the slices are tender throughout, approximately 11–15 minutes (alternatively, the potato slices can be cooked in a 400°F oven for about 15–18 minutes per side). Remove from the oven and set them aside.

4 Meanwhile, place a small nonstick frying pan over medium heat. When the pan is hot, remove from heat and lightly mist it with spray. Return it to the heat and add the egg whites. Once they begin to set slightly, use a large spatula to gently nudge them into the same shape as the sweet potato.

5 Add the bacon strips side by side in the pan so they don't touch each other or the egg. Flip the egg to fully cook it. When the egg is fully cooked, remove it from the pan, and cover to keep it warm. Continue cooking the bacon, flipping it once, until it is crisp, about 3–5 minutes per side. Transfer the bacon to a paper towel–lined plate to remove any excess bacon grease.

6 Place one piece of sweet potato on a plate. Top it with the egg, bacon, and then the arugula. Place the second slice of sweet potato on top to create a sandwich.

CHOICES/EXCHANGES
1 ½ starch, 1 lean protein

PER SERVING
180 calories, 3 g fat, 1 g saturated fat, 0 g trans fat, 10 mg cholesterol, 420 mg sodium, 585 mg potassium, 21 g carbohydrate, 4 g fiber, 7 g sugars, 16 g protein, 20 mg phosphorus

Summer California Breakfast Sandwich

Olive oil spray (propellant free)

2 large egg whites (preferably cage free)

1 (1 ounce) slice turkey bacon (preferably natural and nitrate free), cut in half crosswise

1 spelt or sprouted grain or gluten free English muffin (preferably natural)

¼ medium avocado, cut into 3 slices

1 large (or 3 small) very thin tomato slices

1 Place a medium nonstick frying pan over medium high heat. When the pan is hot, remove from heat just long enough to lightly mist with spray. Off to one side, add the egg whites to the pan. As the egg begins to set slightly, use a silicone spatula to shape it into a rough 4 inch circle.

2 Lay the bacon strips side by side next to the egg so they do not touch. Allow the egg to set completely on the bottom, then flip and continue cooking until the egg is set throughout. Remove egg from the pan and cover on a plate to keep warm. Continue cooking the bacon until desired crispness is reached, about 1–2 minutes per side.

3 Meanwhile, separate the halves of the English muffin and toast them.

4 Place the bottom half of the English muffin on a plate. Add the avocado, the egg, the tomato, and then the bacon strips side by side. Cover the sandwich with the English muffin top. Enjoy immediately.

Cook's Notes

I use spelt English muffins because they are the leanest and lightest of the whole grain options I've found. Be sure to read the nutrition labels of all options you're considering. Don't be "tricked" when reading labels, especially when it comes to gluten free English muffins. Most English muffin packages list a whole muffin as one serving, but I've noticed a few gluten free ones that are higher in calories and list a ½ muffin as a serving—who eats just half of an English muffin?!

If you want the eggs to be a perfect circle, use a 4 inch diameter cookie cutter. Be sure to spray the inside of the cookie cutter with olive oil spray so the egg doesn't stick.

CHOICES/EXCHANGES
1 starch, 1 nonstarchy vegetable, 1 lean protein, 1 fat

PER SERVING
190 calories, 8 g fat, 1 g saturated fat, 0 g trans fat, 10 mg cholesterol, 430 mg sodium, 350 mg potassium, 20 g carbohydrate, 3 g fiber, 2 g sugars, 14 g protein, 15 mg phosphorus

SUMMER CALIFORNIA BREAKFAST SANDWICH

"Fried Egg" Topped Avocado Toast

Fresno peppers, if you're not familiar with them, are not as spicy as jalapeños. If you have trouble finding Fresno peppers in the grocery store, you can substitute jalapeños, just make sure you don't use as many. If you like spicy, keep the pepper seeds in the dish. If not, make sure not to include them. Don't know how to seed peppers? Visit www.devinalexander.com/diabetes and I'll show you!

½ medium ripe avocado (about ¼ cup)

½ teaspoon freshly squeezed lime juice

1 tablespoon finely chopped Fresno peppers (red chili peppers), or more to taste

3 large egg whites (preferably cage free)

Olive oil spray (propellant free)

¾ ounce finely shredded extra light sharp cheddar cheese (preferably natural)

1 slice sprouted grain bread

1 In a small bowl, using a fork, lightly mash the avocado just enough so that it will spread across a slice of bread (but leave some chunks). Stir in the lime juice and set aside.

2 In a small bowl, stir the peppers into the egg whites.

3 Place a small nonstick frying pan over medium heat. When hot, remove it from heat just long enough to mist it with spray. Add the egg and pepper mixture. As the egg starts to set, after about 1–2 minutes, use a spatula to form it into a "fried egg" relatively the same size as the piece of bread. When the underside of the egg is completely set, flip the egg with a large spatula, doing your best to retain its shape.

4 Add the cheese evenly over the top of the egg. Continue cooking until the egg is set through and the cheese is melted, about 1–3 minutes.

5 Meanwhile, toast the bread to a light golden brown. Place the bread on a plate. Spread the avocado evenly over it. Place the cooked cheesy egg on top. Enjoy immediately.

CHOICES/EXCHANGES
1 starch, 3 lean protein, ½ fat

PER SERVING
240 calories, 8 g fat, 2 g saturated fat, 0 g trans fat, 10 mg cholesterol, 400 mg sodium, 375 mg potassium, 19 g carbohydrate, 6 g fiber, 2 g sugars, 23 g protein, 40 mg phosphorus

Roasted Cherry Tomato Topped Goat Cheese Omelet

I cook breakfast almost every morning that I'm not on the road. And my breakfasts generally involve egg whites in some way. I love to couple this omelet with a greens drink like my Pineapple Greens Juice (see page 18) or Happy Tummy Greens Juice (see page 17) to start my day off right.

8 cherry tomatoes, stems removed if necessary

½ teaspoon extra virgin olive oil

¼ teaspoon freshly minced garlic

1/16 teaspoon sea salt

Freshly ground black pepper, to taste, if desired

4 large egg whites (preferably cage free)

1 tablespoon finely chopped fresh flat leaf parsley

Olive oil spray (propellant free)

½ ounce (about 2 tablespoons) crumbled light goat cheese (preferably natural)

½ tablespoon slivered fresh basil leaves (aka basil chiffonade)

1 Preheat the oven to 400°F. Line a small baking sheet with nonstick foil.

2 Add the tomatoes to a small mixing bowl along with the oil, garlic, salt, and pepper. Using a rubber spatula, gently mix them until the tomatoes are evenly coated. Place them on the prepared baking sheet and roast them in the oven until they shrink in size and the skins crack slightly, about 7–10 minutes.

3 Meanwhile, add the egg whites and parsley to a medium bowl. Beat them lightly with a fork until combined.

4 Lightly mist a small nonstick frying pan with spray and place it over medium heat. Add the egg mixture. Cook the egg until it is set on the bottom. Flip it and add the cheese evenly over half of the egg. Continue cooking the omelet until the egg is completely set, about 2–5 minutes. Carefully flip the bare half of the egg over the other half. Transfer the omelet to a serving plate.

5 Mound the roasted tomatoes in the center of the omelet and top with basil. Enjoy immediately.

CHOICES/EXCHANGES
1 nonstarchy vegetable, 2 lean protein, ½ fat

PER SERVING
150 calories, 6 g fat, 2.5 g saturated fat, 0 g trans fat, 5 mg cholesterol, 430 mg sodium, 570 mg potassium, 7 g carbohydrate, 2 g fiber, 5 g sugars, 19 g protein, 95 mg phosphorus

Scrambled Eggs with Sautéed Shrimp

Years ago, I had brunch at the Bryant Park Grill in New York City. They had the most beautiful and scrumptious dish (I don't remember the exact name, but it was something like Scrambled Eggs with Grilled Jumbo Prawns and Fresh Tomato Slices). They placed a tower of scrambled eggs (or in my case, scrambled egg whites) in the center of the plate. Perfectly grilled jumbo prawns hung from it and fresh tomato slices circled the plate. It was so memorable both because I'd never really realized how much I could enjoy shrimp with eggs before, and also because it just looked so good. Having thought about how to duplicate it, I created this twist on the flavor combo, and have been in love with it ever since.

Olive oil spray (propellant free)

4 large egg whites (preferably cage free)

3 ounces medium (31–40 count) shrimp (preferably wild caught), peeled and deveined

½ teaspoon extra virgin olive oil

¾ teaspoon freshly minced garlic

½ cup fresh pico de gallo or fresh salsa (look for it in the refrigerator section)

1 ½ teaspoons finely chopped fresh cilantro leaves

Freshly ground black pepper, to taste, if desired

1 Lightly mist a medium microwave safe bowl with spray. Add the egg whites. Set aside.

2 Toss the shrimp with the olive oil in a small mixing bowl.

3 Preheat a small nonstick frying pan over medium high heat. Remove the pan from the heat just long enough to lightly mist it with spray. Place the garlic and shrimp in the pan and cook, stirring frequently, until the shrimp are bright pink and cooked through, 2–3 minutes.

4 Meanwhile, place a microwave safe plate over the bowl of egg whites and microwave the egg whites on low for 30 seconds. Continue microwaving them in 30 second intervals until they are just a bit runny on top. Then stir them with a fork, breaking them apart into large pieces. By the time you "scramble" and stir them, the residual heat should have cooked away the runniness. If they are still undercooked, microwave them on low in 10 second intervals until just done.

5 Add the eggs to the pan with the shrimp. Gently stir the eggs into the shrimp mixture until they are well combined. Transfer the shrimp and eggs to a serving plate or bowl and top them with the pico de gallo and cilantro. Season them with pepper. Enjoy immediately.

CHOICES/EXCHANGES
2 nonstarchy vegetable, 3 lean protein

PER SERVING
200 calories, 4 g fat, 0.5 g saturated fat, 0 g trans fat, 130 mg cholesterol, 410 mg sodium, 385 mg potassium, 10 g carbohydrate, 0 g fiber, 1 g sugars, 32 g protein, 200 mg phosphorus

SCRAMBLED EGGS WITH SAUTÉED SHRIMP

Weekday Morning Bruschetta Topped Eggs

This is one of my go to breakfast dishes. It's so light and so flavorful! Pair it with a greens juice for a super light breakfast, or if you're in more of an indulgent mood, you can always follow it with my German Chocolate Overnight Oats (see page 14).

Olive oil spray (propellant free)

4 large egg whites (preferably cage free)

Freshly ground black pepper, to taste, if desired

¼ cup Body Lovin' Bruschetta (see page 188)

*If you have the Body Lovin' Bruschetta prepared.

1 Lightly mist a large (about 4 ½ inch diameter) microwave safe ramekin with spray (you can use a microwave safe mug if you don't have a ramekin). Add the egg whites. Place a microwave safe plate over top (to keep the eggs from splattering) and microwave for 30 seconds on high heat. Continue microwaving the eggs in 15 second intervals until they are just a bit runny on top. Then, using a fork, stir them to break them into large "scrambled" pieces. By the time you "scramble" them, the residual heat should have cooked away the runniness. If they are still undercooked, cook them in 15 second intervals until no liquid remains.

2 Wait about 10 seconds after cooking to make sure the eggs are completely cooked and no moisture remains. Season them with pepper. Top eggs with the bruschetta. Enjoy immediately.

Cook's Notes

Prep time is a breeze when the bruschetta is premade.

CHOICES/EXCHANGES
1 nonstarchy vegetable, 2 lean protein

PER SERVING
110 calories, 3.5 g fat, 0.5 g saturated fat, 0 g trans fat, 0 mg cholesterol, 370 mg sodium, 370 mg potassium, 4 g carbohydrate, 1 g fiber, 3 g sugars, 15 g protein, 35 mg phosphorus

Bacon, Egg & Cheese Breakfast Salad

While I always recommend that you prep all of your ingredients before you begin cooking, it's particularly important with this recipe. If you do, you're more likely to ensure a crisp salad with a warm egg, which is how this recipe is best enjoyed. The average person probably wants a full tablespoon of dressing on this salad. But if you're someone (like me) who prefers less dressing, you may find that 2 teaspoons is enough here; consider starting with 2 teaspoons, tasting, and adding the additional teaspoon if desired.

Olive oil spray (propellant free)

3 large egg whites (preferably cage free)

3 cups loosely packed torn arugula leaves

1 slice center cut bacon (preferably nitrate free), cut in half crosswise

1 tablespoon Rockin' Body Balsamic (see page 185)

⅛ cup chopped sweet onion (chopped into slivers)

1 tablespoon shredded Parmesan cheese (preferably natural)

Freshly ground black pepper, to taste, if desired

*If you have the Rockin' Body Balsamic prepared.

1 Mist a standard ramekin (about 3 ½ inches in diameter) with spray. Add the egg whites. Set them aside.

2 Place the arugula in a bowl big enough to toss it. Set it aside.

3 Place a medium nonstick frying pan over medium high heat. Lay the bacon strips side by side so they don't touch. Cook for 1 minute, then turn and cook for another 1–2 minutes until they are cooked to the desired crispness (about 3–4 minutes total). Cut the bacon into small pieces and set aside.

4 Meanwhile, microwave the egg whites in 15 second intervals until they are set through, about 45 seconds to 1 ½ minutes.

5 Add the dressing, onions, and half of the bacon to the arugula and toss until well combined. Transfer the salad to a serving plate. Place the cooked egg in the center of the arugula. Sprinkle the remaining bacon over top, followed by the cheese. Season with pepper. Enjoy immediately.

CHOICES/EXCHANGES
1 nonstarchy vegetable, 2 lean protein

PER SERVING
160 calories, 8 g fat, 2.5 g saturated fat, 0 g trans fat, 10 mg cholesterol, 410 mg sodium, 420 mg potassium, 7 g carbohydrate, 1 g fiber, 4 g sugars, 17 g protein, 50 mg phosphorus

GINGERBREAD OVERNIGHT OATS

Gingerbread Overnight Oats

A lot of people find it really tough to fit a nourishing breakfast into their day. Well, these overnight oats are the perfect solution! Not only are they delicious, but one serving has as much protein as eating a 4 ounce chicken breast, and supplies good fat, omega 3 fatty acids, and 8 g of fiber. Prepare this breakfast in the evening, and you won't find yourself tempted to grab a sugary muffin or hit the drive thru the next morning, even if your morning becomes unexpectedly busy!

½ cup old fashioned oats

½ scoop (15 grams) stevia sweetened vanilla protein powder

½ cup unsweetened vanilla almond milk

2 teaspoons (8 grams) chia seeds

1 teaspoon molasses

¼ teaspoon vanilla extract

⅛ teaspoon ground cinnamon

1⁄16 teaspoon ground ginger

Pinch ground cloves

Pinch ground nutmeg

1 tablespoon chopped walnuts

1 In a small mixing bowl, mix the oats, protein powder, milk, chia seeds, molasses, vanilla, cinnamon, ginger, cloves, and nutmeg until well combined. Transfer the mixture to a jar or resealable plastic container. Refrigerate overnight.

2 Remove the oatmeal from the refrigerator and top it with walnuts just before enjoying.

Cook's Notes

I've found that protein powders vary widely in taste. Before you use one as an ingredient in a recipe, make sure you find one you like. Some powders have a bad aftertaste, while others literally provide vanilla sweetness. Curious what brands I use? Visit **www.devinalexander.com/diabetes** for more info on my favorite products.

CHOICES/EXCHANGES
2 starch, ½ carbohydrate, 2 lean protein, 1 ½ fat

PER SERVING
350 calories, 11 g fat, 1 g saturated fat, 0 g trans fat, 0 mg cholesterol, 170 mg sodium, 245 mg potassium, 39 g carbohydrate, 8 g fiber, 5 g sugars, 22 g protein, 125 mg phosphorus

German Chocolate Overnight Oats

½ cup old fashioned oats

½ cup unsweetened vanilla almond milk

½ tablespoon zero calorie natural sweetener

½ tablespoon unsweetened cocoa powder

1 tablespoon unsweetened, reduced fat shredded coconut

1 tablespoon chopped pecans

1 Combine the rolled oats, almond milk, sweetener, cocoa powder, and coconut in an 8 ounce jar or resealable plastic container. Refrigerate the oatmeal mixture for at least 6 hours (or up to 2 days).

2 Remove oatmeal from the refrigerator and top with the pecans just before enjoying.

Cook's Notes

Using 1 tablespoon of a stevia brown sugar blend (such as Truvia Brown Sugar Blend) in this recipe instead of pure stevia or another zero calorie natural sweetner makes it truly taste like a German chocolate treat. It's yummy enough for dessert, but it also adds 5 g of sugar per serving. You can make a few servings with the brown sugar blend and keep them in the refrigerator for a few days to have on hand when a chocolate craving hits. For breakfast, I'd recommend sticking with a zero calorie natural sweetener.

CHOICES/EXCHANGES
2 starch, ½ carbohydrate, 2 fat

PER SERVING
280 calories, 12 g fat, 2.6 g saturated fat, 0 g trans fat, 0 mg cholesterol, 95 mg sodium, 350 mg potassium, 37 g carbohydrate, 8 g fiber, 1 g sugars, 9 g protein, 285 mg phosphorus

Chocolate Almond Zoats

Zoats (aka zucchini oats) have become very trendy in the U.S. in the last year or so. And why not? Zucchini is so mild in flavor that you really can't taste it. It bulks up your oatmeal, giving you a big serving with few added calories and lots of added fiber. If you leave the peel on the zucchini, as I do here, you also get some soluble fiber, which is known to slow down digestion...plus, you'll stay fuller longer. This is an extra "win" for anyone living with diabetes.

½ cup finely shredded zucchini

½ cup old fashioned oats

1 cup unsweetened vanilla almond milk

½ tablespoon unsweetened cocoa powder

½ tablespoon zero calorie natural sweetener

¼ teaspoon vanilla extract

⅛ teaspoon almond extract

1/16 teaspoon sea salt

½ tablespoon stevia sweetened dark chocolate chips or dark chocolate pieces

1 ½ tablespoons dry roasted almonds, roughly chopped

1 Place the zucchini in a lint free towel, and wring as much liquid from it as possible.

2 Transfer the zucchini to a small soup pot. Add the oats and the milk. Cook them over medium heat, stirring the mixture frequently with a rubber spatula or wooden spoon, until the moisture has evaporated, 4–7 minutes on a gas burner (longer on an electric).

3 Remove the pan from the heat and stir in the cocoa powder, sweetener, vanilla extract, almond extract, and salt until well combined. Add the chocolate chips and stir them until just evenly distributed—don't completely melt them.

4 Transfer the zoats to a serving bowl and top them with the almonds. Enjoy immediately.

Cook's Notes

You definitely want to shred your zucchini finely. If you do, it is more likely to be undetectable, especially when combined with other flavors.

CHOICES/EXCHANGES
2 starch, ½ carbohydrate, 2 ½ fat

PER SERVING
300 calories, 14 g fat, 2.7 g saturated fat, 0 g trans fat, 0 mg cholesterol, 320 mg sodium, 670 mg potassium, 37 g carbohydrate, 9 g fiber, 3 g sugars, 10 g protein, 300 mg phosphorus

Chocolate Sweet Cherry Zoats

When making zoats, it's important to use a fine shredder to shred your zucchini. If not, you might find the texture unappealing. It's not necessary to peel the zucchini before shredding it; in fact, it's better for you if you don't. Just trim and discard the ends and use the fine shredding side of a box grater, being careful not to cut yourself as you get close to the end of the zucchini.

½ cup finely shredded zucchini

½ cup old fashioned oats

1 cup unsweetened vanilla almond milk

½ cup frozen tart cherries, defrosted and quartered

½ tablespoon unsweetened cocoa powder

1 teaspoon zero calorie natural sweetener

¼ teaspoon vanilla extract

⅛ teaspoon almond extract

1/16 teaspoon sea salt

½ tablespoon stevia sweetened dark chocolate chips or dark chocolate pieces

1 Place the zucchini in a lint free towel, and wring the towel to remove as much moisture as possible.

2 Transfer the drained zucchini to a small saucepan. Mix in the oats. Pour the almond milk into the pan. Cook the mixture over medium heat, using a rubber spatula or wooden spoon to stir the mixture frequently, until the moisture has evaporated, about 4–7 minutes on a gas burner (longer on an electric).

3 Remove the pan from the heat. Stir in the cherries, cocoa powder, sweetener, vanilla extract, almond extract, and salt until well combined. Add the chocolate chips and stir them until just evenly distributed—don't completely melt them. Enjoy immediately.

CHOICES/EXCHANGES
2 starch, ½ fruit, ½ carbohydrate, 1½ fat

PER SERVING
330 calories, 9 g fat, 2.3 g saturated fat, 0 g trans fat, 0 mg cholesterol, 320 mg sodium, 730 mg potassium, 45 g carbohydrate, 9 g fiber, 9 g sugars, 9 g protein, 275 mg phosphorus

Happy Tummy Greens Juice

Parsley and ginger are known to settle a sick stomach and to help keep a healthy stomach in good shape. That's why this refreshing juice is called Happy Tummy Greens Juice. I served this green juice in my restaurant and it was always a big hit, even among the vacation crowd, as a refreshing way to start the morning.

1 medium (about 5–6 ounce) Granny Smith apple, cored and seeded

⅓ medium cucumber (about 3 ounces), ends trimmed

¾ inch cube (about ⅓ ounce) fresh ginger

1 ½ cups packed fresh spinach leaves

½ cup fresh parsley leaves (some stems are okay)

6 ice cubes

1 Cut the apple, cucumber, and ginger into quarters. Add them to the jar/pitcher of a blender along with the spinach, parsley, and ice cubes. Blend all ingredients on high for a few seconds until the ingredients start to incorporate.

2 Using a spatula, scrape down the sides of the blender, as needed, and continue to blend the mixture until it is completely smooth.

3 Transfer the juice to a 14–16 ounce glass. Garnish with a cucumber slice, if desired. Enjoy immediately.

CHOICES/EXCHANGES
1 fruit, 2 nonstarchy vegetable

PER SERVING
110 calories, 1 g fat, 0.2 g saturated fat, 0 g trans fat, 0 mg cholesterol, 80 mg sodium, 870 mg potassium, 25 g carbohydrate, 6 g fiber, 14 g sugars, 4 g protein, 90 mg phosphorus

Pineapple Greens Juice

Pineapple is one of my favorite additions to greens juices. It's so sweet and tropical! I find myself staying the most fit when I pair this juice with an egg white dish for breakfast. The greens juice provides nutrients that help curb my cravings and the protein in the egg whites helps me feel full, making them the perfect combo.

*You can strain the pulp from this juice, but I wouldn't recommend doing so. When you strain the pulp or make the drink using a juicer (as opposed to a blender), you lose the fiber in the ingredients. That being said, it's important to have a good, high powered blender in order to get the ideal consistency for your greens juices. If you're curious about some of my favorite brands, check out **www.devinalexander.com/diabetes** to learn what equipment I use and so much more.*

2 stalks celery, ends trimmed
(no need to trim away leaves)
and cut into thirds crosswise

1 cup frozen unsweetened
pineapple chunks

¾ cup packed parsley leaves
(some stems can remain, just
trim the ends)

½ medium cucumber (or ⅓ medium
English cucumber), ends trimmed
and cut into quarters

¾ cup packed fresh spinach leaves

1 Add the celery, pineapple, parsley, cucumber, and spinach to the jar/pitcher of a blender. Pulse the mixture a few times then blend it on high speed until it is completely smooth.

2 Garnish each serving with a pineapple wedge, if desired. Enjoy immediately.

Cook's Notes

If your blender isn't very powerful, you may need to add a tiny bit of liquid to blend the juice. I recommend adding a hint of 100% pineapple juice.

CHOICES/EXCHANGES
½ fruit, 1 nonstarchy vegetable

PER SERVING
70 calories, 0 g fat, 0 g saturated fat, 0 g trans fat, 0 mg cholesterol, 85 mg sodium, 445 mg potassium, 16 g carbohydrate, 4 g fiber, 10 g sugars, 2 g protein, 20 mg phosphorus

Pumpkin Pie Smoothie

⅔ cup canned pumpkin purée

⅓ cup 100% liquid egg whites (preferably cage free)

¼ cup silken tofu (liquid drained before measuring)

1 teaspoon vanilla extract

¼–½ teaspoon maple extract

2 ½ teaspoons zero calorie natural sweetener

½ teaspoon pumpkin pie spice

½ teaspoon ground cinnamon

6 ice cubes

1 Add the pumpkin, egg whites, tofu, vanilla extract, maple extract, sweetener, pumpkin pie spice, cinnamon, and ice cubes to the jar/pitcher of a blender. Blend on high speed until smooth, stopping the blender intermittently to scrape down the sides as needed.

2 Pour the smoothie into a 12–14 ounce glass. Enjoy immediately.

Cook's Notes

It is important that you use 100% liquid egg whites from a carton, not actual egg whites for this recipe and any others in which you're consuming a raw egg product. The whites in the carton are pasteurized and safe to eat raw, while egg whites from whole eggs are not, and it's too easy to get salmonella from consuming raw egg.

I personally prefer to use ½ teaspoon of maple extract in this recipe instead of ¼ teaspoon, though the majority of my recipe testing team preferred ¼ teaspoon of maple extract. But I like maple flavor more than the taste of cloves (part of the pumpkin spice blend). I recommend starting with ¼ teaspoon of maple extract the first time you make the recipe, then increasing the amount if desired.

CHOICES/EXCHANGES

1 starch, 2 lean protein

PER SERVING

160 calories, 2.5 g fat, 0.6 g saturated fat, 0 g trans fat, 0 mg cholesterol, 170 mg sodium, 610 mg potassium, 18 g carbohydrate, 6 g fiber, 8 g sugars, 15 g protein, 130 mg phosphorus

Sandwiches, Burgers & Pizzas

BBQ Beef Sandwich

When buying a barbecue sauce, compare labels. Look for one that isn't too high in sugar. I wouldn't recommend opting for a "low carb" barbecue sauce if it's full of chemicals, but it's best to buy one that has no more than 7–10 g of carbohydrate per serving. Want to know more about products I'm using? Visit me at **www.devinalexander.com/diabetes** *and I'll tell you!*

1 tablespoon whole grain oat flour

¼ teaspoon garlic powder

⅛ teaspoon onion powder

1 pound trimmed top round roast or steak, cut into ¾ inch cubes

Olive oil spray (propellant free)

¾ cup low sodium beef broth

2 tablespoons liquid smoke (preferably natural)

2 cups white onion strips

¼ cup plus 2 tablespoons barbecue sauce, divided (look for one that's relatively low in sugar)

4 whole grain hamburger buns

1 In a medium plastic resealable bag, combine the flour, garlic powder, and onion powder. Add the beef and shake the bag until the beef is evenly coated with the flour mixture. Let the beef rest for 15 minutes, unrefrigerated (though not longer for food safety reasons).

2 Preheat a medium nonstick soup pot over medium high heat. When it's hot, lightly mist the pan with spray then add the beef. Brown the beef on all sides, about 1 minute per side, then turn the heat to medium and add the broth and liquid smoke. When the liquid comes to a boil, reduce the heat to low (the liquid should still be boiling slightly). Cover and cook the beef, stirring occasionally, for 1–1 ½ hours or until it's very tender (the pieces should easily fall apart when smashed with a fork).

3 During the last 10 minutes of the beef cooking, lightly mist a small nonstick frying pan with spray, and place it over medium heat. Add the onions and cook them until tender, about 5–8 minutes.

4 Using a slotted spoon, drain the beef of any excess liquid and transfer it to a medium bowl. Using a fork, separate the pieces so the beef is somewhat shredded then mix in ¼ cup of the barbecue sauce.

5 Meanwhile, place the bun halves, insides down, in a medium nonstick frying pan over medium heat (no need to add oil). Cook them until just toasted, about 2–4 minutes.

6 Place each bun bottom on a plate. Pile about ½ cup of the beef mixture onto each bun. Top with one quarter of the onions (about ¼ cup) and drizzle the remaining barbecue sauce evenly among them. Add the bun tops and serve immediately.

CHOICES/EXCHANGES
1 ½ starch, ½ carbohydrate, 1 nonstarchy vegetable, 3 lean protein

PER SERVING
300 calories, 6 g fat, 1.7 g saturated fat, 0 g trans fat, 60 mg cholesterol, 420 mg sodium, 490 mg potassium, 33 g carbohydrate, 4 g fiber, 9 g sugars, 29 g protein, 275 mg phosphorus

BBQ BEEF SANDWICH

Cranberry Aioli Turkey Sandwich

People often think of turkey as being difficult to cook because they only do it at Thanksgiving (or watch others spend days creating a Thanksgiving feast). However, it's a myth that turkey is time consuming to prepare. While making a stuffing for turkey is super labor intensive if you're making it from scratch, throwing an unstuffed bird into the oven takes mere minutes. I cook turkey all the time, year round, so I have lean and very clean deli meats to make sandwiches just like this one. And making turkey breasts is even easier. Plus, it saves me a lot of money over buying it from the deli counter.

1 whole wheat sandwich slim or thin (no more than 100 calories and 150 mg sodium)

1 tablespoon fruit juice–sweetened cranberry preserves

½ tablespoon light mayonnaise

¼ teaspoon dried rosemary leaves, or more to taste

4 ounces Sriracha Mayo Roasted Turkey Breast (see page 92)

1 leaf red or green leaf lettuce

*If you have the Sriracha Mayo Roasted Turkey Breast prepared.

1 Place the bottom of the sandwich slim/thin on a plate. Spread the cranberry preserves then mayo evenly over it. Sprinkle the rosemary over that.

2 Pile the turkey evenly on top. Add the lettuce leaf.

3 Top the sandwich with the sandwich slim/thin top and enjoy immediately or wrap the sandwich tightly in plastic wrap and refrigerate until ready to serve.

CHOICES/EXCHANGES
1 ½ starch, ½ fruit, 4 lean protein

PER SERVING
330 calories, 7 g fat, 1.1 g saturated fat, 0 g trans fat, 90 mg cholesterol, 420 mg sodium, 420 mg potassium, 32 g carbohydrate, 5 g fiber, 12 g sugars, 38 g protein, 345 mg phosphorus

Fat Burner Sandwich

I originally wrote a version of this sandwich recipe for Muscle & Fitness *magazine at their request to compile a sandwich with ingredients known to support burning fat. I've been enjoying this even leaner adaptation ever since. Though it appears pretty basic, the combination of ingredients—particularly the addition of watercress and the sriracha on the turkey—not only provides a hearty midday meal, but is sure to fill you up and provide metabolic support. Who doesn't want that? Plus, it has a small fraction of the sodium found in traditional deli meat sandwiches. It's not at all uncommon for 4 ounces of lean turkey from the deli to have 1,000 mg of sodium or more, while some breads have 150–200 mg of sodium per slice! This same sandwich from the deli counter would likely have as many as 1,600 mg of sodium!*

1 whole grain or multigrain sandwich slim or thin (preferably natural)

2 teaspoons Chinese hot mustard or Dijon mustard, or more to taste, if desired

½ cup watercress leaves

4 ounces Sriracha Mayo Roasted Turkey Breast (see page 92) or other extra lean, low sodium turkey slices

½ ounce sliced or shredded reduced fat Swiss cheese (preferably natural)

*If you have the Sriracha Mayo Roasted Turkey Breast prepared.

1 Place the bottom of the sandwich slim/thin on a plate. Spread the mustard evenly over it.

2 Add the watercress, then the turkey, then the cheese. Enjoy immediately or wrap the sandwich tightly in plastic wrap and refrigerate to enjoy up to 1 day later.

Cook's Notes

When you're buying sandwich slims/thins, be sure to read the labels of each brand. I've found that they vary widely in terms of nutrition. I found one variety with as little as 135 mg of sodium, 1 g of sugar, and only 90 calories per slim/thin. However, some have as many as 170 calories, 4 g of sugar, and 230 mg of sodium per serving.

CHOICES/EXCHANGES
1½ starch, 5 lean protein

PER SERVING
320 calories, 8 g fat, 2.2 g saturated fat, 0 g trans fat, 100 mg cholesterol, 490 mg sodium, 470 mg potassium, 22 g carbohydrate, 5 g fiber, 3 g sugars, 44 g protein, 445 mg phosphorus

Grilled Chicken Sandwich with Pesto & Roasted Red Pepper

1 pound trimmed boneless, skinless chicken breasts (preferably free range), pounded to ½ inch thickness

Olive oil spray (propellant free)

⅛ teaspoon reduced sodium salt substitute

Freshly ground black pepper, to taste

1 (8 ounce) multigrain or whole wheat baguette

½ cup Creamy Carrot Top Pesto (see page 183)

1 ⅓ cups arugula leaves

1 medium (6 ounce) heirloom tomato, cut into thin slices

⅓ cup very thin red onion slices

1 small (about 5 ounce) roasted red bell pepper, core and seeds removed and cut into slivers (about ⅓ cup)

*If you have the Creamy Carrot Top Pesto prepared.

1 Preheat a grill to high.

2 Mist the chicken on both sides with spray. Season it with the salt substitute and pepper.

3 Reduce the grill heat to medium, if possible, or select a place away from direct flame and lay the chicken breasts on the grill. Grill the chicken until it is no longer pink inside, about 2–5 minutes per side.

4 Turn the baguette on its side and cut the entire length, not cutting all the way through, as you would cut a roll to make a sandwich. Open it carefully, being sure not to break apart the 2 halves. Spread the pesto evenly over the top half of the inside of the baguette.

5 Cut the grilled chicken breasts in half or in thirds (not into strips), to make them better cover the length of the baguette. Place the breast pieces evenly in the baguette. Top the chicken evenly with the arugula, tomato slices, onions, and red peppers. Close the baguette and cut it crosswise into 4 equal sandwiches. Enjoy immediately.

Cook's Notes

These sandwiches make a great packed lunch, and I love serving them at parties. To turn the whole sandwich into a party sub, secure the filled baguette with toothpicks placed about 1 inch apart stuck through the sandwich from top to bottom. Then, using a serrated knife, cut between the toothpicks to create many snack sized pieces.

When you shop for a baguette, look for one that's long and thin. If you can only find a 12 ounce baguette that's really dense, you can pull some of the bread out of the center to make it 8 ounces.

Roast the red pepper yourself instead of using store bought roasted peppers. The ones you buy in the jars at the grocery store are full of sodium, and the freshly roasted ones actually taste better anyway! See Roasted Red Peppers (page 196) to learn how to roast your own.

CHOICES/EXCHANGES
2 starch, 1 nonstarchy vegetable,
3 lean protein, ½ fat

PER SERVING
350 calories, 8 g fat, 1.7 g saturated fat, 0 g trans fat, 65 mg cholesterol, 490 mg sodium, 570 mg potassium, 35 g carbohydrate, 4 g fiber, 6 g sugars, 32 g protein, 370 mg phosphorus

GRILLED CHICKEN SANDWICH WITH PESTO & ROASTED RED PEPPER

California Cobb Grilled Chicken Sandwich

1 (4 ounce) boneless, skinless chicken breast (preferably free range), visible fat trimmed and pounded to ½ inch thickness

Olive oil spray (propellant free)

Freshly ground black pepper, to taste

1 slice center cut bacon (preferably nitrate free)

1 whole grain or multigrain sandwich slim or thin (preferably natural)

⅕ small ripe avocado (scant ¼ cup), cut into 3 slices

1 small handful mixed baby greens

¼ ounce very thin slices red onion, or to taste

1 large or 3 small tomato slice(s)

1 tablespoon yogurt based, store bought blue cheese dressing

1 Preheat a grill to high.

2 Mist the chicken on both sides with spray. Season it with pepper.

3 Reduce grill heat to low, if possible, or select a spot away from direct flame and lay the chicken breast on the grill. Grill the chicken until it is no longer pink inside, 2–5 minutes per side.

4 In the final minutes of grilling the chicken, add the bacon strip to the grill. Add the bun halves, insides face down, to the top rack of the grill (or away from direct flame). Grill the bacon until it's lightly crisped, about 1 minute per side, and the bun halves until they are lightly toasted, about 30 seconds to 1 minute. Chop the bacon slice into very small pieces.

5 Place the bottom of the bun on a plate. Using a fork, slightly mash the avocado slices into the bun. Press the bacon pieces into the avocado evenly across the bun. Add the greens, onion, tomato, and chicken. Spread the dressing over the inside of the bun top and flip it atop the sandwich. Enjoy immediately.

Cook's Notes

Find a sandwich slim or thin, burger bun, or English muffin that you love that is whole grain and has as little sodium as possible. Many people don't realize how much salt is found in most breads and bread products. I found one at my local grocery store with only 90 calories and 135 mg of sodium, so I use that as one of my go to ingredients.

Look for a blue cheese dressing that is yogurt based and is relatively low in calories and sodium. I use one with 35 calories and 135 mg of sodium per 2 tablespoons of dressing. Want to know which brand I'm currently using? Go to **www.devinalexander.com/diabetes**.

CHOICES/EXCHANGES
1 ½ starch, 1 nonstarchy vegetable, 4 lean protein, ½ fat

PER SERVING
350 calories, 11 g fat, 2.7 g saturated fat, 0 g trans fat, 75 mg cholesterol, 480 mg sodium, 655 mg potassium, 29 g carbohydrate, 5 g fiber, 6 g sugars, 35 g protein, 330 mg phosphorus

Curry Chicken Salad Cups

This recipe is great for transforming leftover grilled chicken breasts, or you can always purposefully make a few extra pieces when you are grilling chicken and keep them on hand for recipes like this one. One of the best ways to stick with healthy eating is to keep lean proteins, veggies, and whole grains readily available at all times!

4 ounces Have-On-Hand Grilled Chicken (see page 192), coarsely chopped

¼ cup ¼ inch cucumber pieces, or to taste

¼ cup ¼ inch mango pieces

1 ½ tablespoons light mayonnaise

¼ teaspoon lime zest

1 teaspoon jarred tandoori paste or red curry paste

2 small iceberg lettuce leaves

¼ cup red onion slivers

*If you have the Have-On-Hand Grilled Chicken prepared.

1 Place the chicken, cucumber, and mango in a medium bowl. Add the mayonnaise, lime zest, and curry paste and stir until well combined.

2 Divide the chicken salad evenly between the 2 lettuce leaves, about 1 cup per leaf. Top each with half the onion. Enjoy immediately.

Cook's Notes

Choose the lowest sodium option when buying tandoori or red curry paste. I used one with 430 mg of sodium per tablespoon.

I recommend that until you are completely familiar with cooking 4 ounce chicken breasts (some people think chicken always takes 20 minutes to cook because they're eating 8 ounce pieces of chicken or they're used to cooking bone in chicken, etc.), you experiment with the cooking time. Cook one breast and cut into it the second you think it might be done to check the color. If there's still pink in the center, continue cooking it and cutting into it every minute until it is done. That way you'll know exactly how long it takes to cook 4 ounces of chicken using your specific oven/grill/etc. The grill I use now is super high powered, so my 4 ounce chicken breasts are always done after 3 minutes of cooking per side. But on my former grill it took 5 minutes per side.

CHOICES/EXCHANGES
½ fruit, 1 nonstarchy vegetable, 3 lean protein, 1 fat

PER SERVING
240 calories, 9 g fat, 1 g saturated fat, 0 g trans fat, 65 mg cholesterol, 460 mg sodium, 445 mg potassium, 12 g carbohydrate, 2 g fiber, 8 g sugars, 27 g protein, 240 mg phosphorus

Greek "Gyro" Sandwich

5 Mediterranean Meatballs (see page 94), reheated if necessary

1 whole wheat pita circle (about 7 inches in diameter), warmed

4 tablespoons Garlicky Dill Dip & Sauce (see page 181)

3 tablespoons fresh mint leaves, cut into thin strips

6 small or 4 large (⅛ inch thick) tomato slices

¼ cup red onion slivers

1 cup baby mixed greens

*If you have the Mediterranean Meatballs and Garlicky Dill Dip & Sauce prepared.

1 Reheat meatballs if necessary. Slice the meatballs into ⅛ inch thick slices.

2 Cut the warmed pita circle in half. Spoon half of the dip into each half and spread it evenly over one side of the inside of the pita. Divide the sliced meatballs, mint, tomato slices, onions, and greens evenly between the two pockets. Serve immediately.

Cook's Notes

I generally reheat meatballs by wrapping them in a foil packet and warming them in a 350°F oven. The pita can be warmed in the same oven directly on an oven rack for a couple minutes. You could also microwave the meatballs or reheat them in a frying pan after slicing, but the oven method tends to keep the meatballs moist and the pita nicely warmed without making it gummy (as the microwave can do).

Look for pita bread that has about 220 calories and 240 mg of sodium or less per circle.

CHOICES/EXCHANGES
1 ½ starch, 1 nonstarchy vegetable, 2 lean protein

PER SERVING
220 calories, 5 g fat, 0.7 g saturated fat, 0 g trans fat, 35 mg cholesterol, 460 mg sodium, 520 mg potassium, 25 g carbohydrate, 6 g fiber, 3 g sugars, 23 g protein, 275 mg phosphorus

GREEK "GYRO" SANDWICH

Pesto Margarita Portobello Burger

Mushrooms are like sponges; when they're run under water, they soak it up. In the process, they lose some amazing flavor (nothing tastes great if it's been waterlogged). So instead of washing the portobello mushroom in this recipe (or any mushrooms), use a mushroom brush to clean them with just a touch of water. You can use a damp paper towel if you don't have a mushroom brush.

"Ugly produce" has become trendy in recent years. Farmers are now selling items (like the heirloom tomatoes used in this recipe) that look a little lopsided or "ugly" but are perfectly delicious. If you're on a budget, you can upgrade your ingredients by turning to ugly produce (for example, buy heirloom tomatoes instead of traditional ones) for greater flavor without greater financial commitment. If you don't see any at your local farmers' market or other places you shop, ask the purveyors if they have any ugly produce. You might find yourself landing a steep discount.

Olive oil spray (propellant free)

1 portobello mushroom (about 2 ¾ ounces)

⅛ teaspoon salt free garlic and herb bread seasoning

Freshly ground black pepper, to taste, if desired

1 (¾ ounce) slice reduced fat provolone cheese (preferably natural)

1 sprouted grain hamburger bun

2 tablespoons Creamy Carrot Top Pesto (see page 183)

3 small or 1 large (¼ inch thick) tomato slices (preferably heirloom tomatoes)

*If you have the Creamy Carrot Top Pesto prepared.

1 Preheat a grill to high.

2 Lightly mist the portobello mushroom with spray and season it with the seasoning and pepper. Place the portobello on the grill, gills side down, and turn the heat to low, if possible, or place it away from direct flame. Grill the mushroom until it is warmed throughout and tender, about 1–3 minutes per side. When you flip the mushroom, top it with the cheese slice.

3 In the last minute of cooking, add the bun halves to the grill, insides face down, away from a direct flame for about 30 seconds to 1 minute. Watch carefully so they don't burn—you just want them very lightly toasted.

4 Place the bun bottom on a plate. Add the grilled portobello, cheese side up. Carefully, using the back of a spoon, spread the pesto over the cheese. Place the tomato slices evenly over top. Top the sandwich with the bun top. Enjoy immediately.

CHOICES/EXCHANGES
2 ½ starch, 1 nonstarchy vegetable, 1 lean protein, 1 fat

PER SERVING
300 calories, 9 g fat, 3 g saturated fat, 0 g trans fat, 15 mg cholesterol, 440 mg sodium, 620 mg potassium, 40 g carbohydrate, 7 g fiber, 3 g sugars, 19 g protein, 360 mg phosphorus

Drippy Taco Burger

It's easy to make a perfect burger patty for this delicious recipe if you lay a sheet of waxed paper over a tortilla, then press the patty on the wax paper until it's slightly larger than half of the tortilla. When pressing the beef, try not to poke your fingertips into it; instead, create a flat surface with your fingers—this will help create a uniformly thick patty.

I originally created a version of this recipe for Men's Fitness *magazine. It was so popular, I adapted it here for ladies to enjoy as well. Want to make it exactly as I make it? Visit me at* **www.devinalexander.com/diabetes** *where I share my pick for the Mexican seasoning and provide chef tips and tricks.*

1 (6 inch) corn tortilla (preferably made with only corn, lime, and salt)

4 ounces 96% lean ground beef (preferably grass fed)

½ teaspoon salt free Mexican seasoning, or more to taste

Olive oil spray (propellant free)

1 leaf green leaf lettuce

3 (⅛ inch thick) slices tomato (about 1 ¼ ounces total)

1 tablespoon sliced jalapeño, or to taste, if desired

1 tablespoon salsa con queso (preferably natural)

2 teaspoons red taco sauce (preferably natural)

1 Preheat a grill to high.

2 Cut a piece of foil that is a bit longer than twice as long as the diameter of the tortilla. Place the tortilla near one edge. Fold the bare side of the foil over the side with the tortilla and enclose the tortilla completely by sealing the edges.

3 In a medium bowl, mix the beef and seasoning until well combined. On a sheet of waxed paper or parchment paper, shape the burger into a half circle patty that is half the size of the tortilla. Then press it even flatter, keeping the general shape so it's about ½ inch bigger than half of the tortilla (the idea being that you want it to fit perfectly on half of the tortilla after it shrinks a bit while cooking). Mist the patty with spray and grill it until desired doneness is reached, about 30 seconds to 1 minute per side for medium rare.

4 Meanwhile, add the wrapped tortilla to the grill for about 1 minute until the tortilla is hot.

5 When the burger is done, being careful not to burn yourself, unwrap the tortilla and place it on a plate. Place the patty over half of the tortilla. Top it with the lettuce, tomatoes, and 1 tablespoon sliced jalapeño, if desired. Then, spread the salsa con queso over the bare half of the tortilla. Drizzle the taco sauce evenly over the filled side. Fold the half with the salsa con queso over the other half. Enjoy immediately.

CHOICES/EXCHANGES
1 starch, 4 lean protein

PER SERVING
250 calories, 8 g fat, 3.4 g saturated fat, 0.3 g trans fat, 70 mg cholesterol, 220 mg sodium, 570 mg potassium, 17 g carbohydrate, 2 g fiber, 2 g sugars, 29 g protein, 340 mg phosphorus

BÁNH MÌ BURGER

Bánh Mì Burger

¼ cup rice wine vinegar

1 tablespoon zero calorie natural sweetener

¼ teaspoon kosher salt

⅛ teaspoon freshly ground black pepper, plus additional to taste, divided

3 radishes, trimmed and cut into matchstick pieces (about ⅓ cup)

1 small carrot, peeled and cut into matchstick pieces (about ⅔ cup)

2 pieces whole grain or multigrain baguette (2 ounces each)

8 ounces 96% lean ground beef (preferably grass fed)

¼ cup (⅛ inch thick) English cucumber slices (about 1 ½ ounces)

¼ cup fresh cilantro leaves

12 very thin slices jalapeño (rounds; about ½ ounce total)

2 teaspoons sriracha (preferably natural), or less to taste

1 Preheat a grill to high.

2 In a deep small bowl or storage container, combine the vinegar, ¼ cup of water, sweetener, salt, ⅛ teaspoon pepper, radishes, and carrots. Set aside.

3 Cut open the baguettes all the way through (sandwich style).

4 On a sheet of parchment paper or waxed paper, shape the beef into 2 equal patties that are about ½ inch larger in area than the size of one baguette piece (burgers will shrink when cooked, so if you make them slightly larger, they will fit perfectly after cooking). Season the patties with additional pepper, if desired. Grill patties on high until desired doneness is reached, about 1–2 minutes per side for medium rare.

5 Meanwhile, add the baguette pieces to the grill, insides face down, away from a direct flame for about 30 seconds to 1 minute. Watch carefully so they don't burn—you just want them very lightly toasted.

6 Place one bottom piece of baguette on each of two plates. Add a burger patty to each. Top each patty evenly with the cucumber, cilantro, and jalapeños.

7 Drain the carrots and radishes from the pickling liquid. Divide them evenly among the burgers. Drizzle each burger with sriracha and top with the baguette tops. Enjoy immediately.

Cook's Notes

If you use a mandolin to cut the carrots and radishes into matchsticks, this burger comes together in just minutes. Don't have a mandolin? Visit me at www.devinalexander.com/diabetes and I'll show you why you might want to invest in one and share my favorite!

Did you know that rice wine vinegar and rice vinegar are the same thing? Just be sure you buy a rice vinegar that is unseasoned for this recipe; it should have 0 calories and 0 g of sugar. The seasoned ones, however, can have as many as 120 calories and may have added sugars.

CHOICES/EXCHANGES
2 starch, 1 nonstarchy vegetable, 3 lean protein

PER SERVING
320 calories, 6 g fat, 2.4 g saturated fat, 0.3 g trans fat, 65 mg cholesterol, 530 mg sodium, 620 mg potassium, 34 g carbohydrate, 3 g fiber, 5 g sugars, 32 g protein, 375 mg phosphorus

Caramelized Sweet Onion Balsamic Burger

Did you know that some brands of balsamic vinegar have added sugars in them? I know a lot of people think that balsamic vinegar has zero calories, but that is generally not the case. They tend to range between 5 and 20 calories per tablespoon and some contain a significant amount of sugar. An average balsamic vinegar has about 14 calories with 3 g of sugars per tablespoon, whereas some other vinegars, such as cider or white vinegar, have almost no calories or sugar. Check labels when choosing a balsamic vinegar for this recipe.

Olive oil spray (propellant free)

½ medium sweet onion (about 5 ounces or 1 cup), cut into ¼ inch squares

⅛ teaspoon reduced sodium salt substitute

Freshly ground black pepper, to taste

2 tablespoons balsamic vinegar

1 teaspoon finely crumbled dried rosemary leaves (crumbled with your fingers)

⅛ teaspoon sea salt

8 ounces 96% lean ground beef (preferably grass fed)

2 sandwich slims or thins (preferably natural)

⅔ cup loosely packed arugula leaves

1 Preheat a grill to high.

2 Mist a small nonstick soup pot with spray. Add the onions, salt substitute, and the pepper and place the pot over medium heat. Cover the pot and cook the onions, stirring them every minute or so, until they barely start to brown and are tender, about 8–12 minutes.

3 Add the balsamic vinegar. Continue cooking the onions, uncovered, stirring occasionally, until the onions are coated and most of the liquid has cooked away, about 1–3 minutes.

4 Meanwhile, in a small bowl, using a fork, mix the rosemary and sea salt into the beef until well combined. Shape the beef into 2 equal patties about 4 ½ inches in diameter. Season the patties with pepper. Grill the patties on high until desired doneness is reached, about 2–3 minutes per side for medium rare.

5 Add the sandwich slim/thin halves, insides face down, to the grill away from a direct flame for about 30 seconds to 1 minute. Watch carefully so they don't burn—you just want them very lightly toasted.

6 Place one sandwich slim/thin bottom on each of two plates. Divide the arugula evenly among the sandwich slims/thins. Top the arugula with the burger patties, then half of the onions (about 2 tablespoons on each). Enjoy immediately.

Cook's Notes

Yes! It's annoying to read labels! But the good news is that if you do it and then consistently use the same products, it's easy to eat so much more indulgently. Some sandwich slims/thins have as little as 135 mg of sodium while others can have over 250 mg of sodium. Look for sandwich slims or thins with 100 calories or less each and as little sodium as possible. Still not convinced? Or want more tips directly from me? Visit me at **www.devinalexander.com/diabetes** and I'll share my picks!

I love arugula. But if you don't, you can use any dark greens you like. Keep in mind that iceberg and romaine lettuce aren't as nutrient rich as other greens.

CHOICES/EXCHANGES
1 ½ starch, 1 nonstarchy vegetable, 3 lean protein

PER SERVING
300 calories, 6 g fat, 2.2 g saturated fat, 0.3 g trans fat, 65 mg cholesterol, 480 mg sodium, 760 mg potassium, 31 g carbohydrate, 7 g fiber, 8 g sugars, 32 g protein, 345 mg phosphorus

BACON RANCH FLATBREAD PIZZA

Bacon Ranch Flatbread Pizza

1 piece whole wheat lavash

¼ cup plus 2 tablespoons Renovated Ranch (see page 184), divided

1 medium tomato (about 4 ounces), sliced as thinly as possible

½ teaspoon freshly minced garlic

2 slices center cut bacon (preferably nitrate free), cut in half

6 ounces Have-On-Hand Grilled Chicken (see page 192), cut into ½ inch cubes, reheated if necessary

1 ½ tablespoons finely sliced fresh chives

*If you have the Renovated Ranch and Have-On-Hand Grilled Chicken prepared.

1 Preheat the oven to 400°F. Line a baking sheet (large enough to fit the flatbread so that it lays flat) with nonstick foil.

2 Place the flatbread on the prepared baking sheet. Crisp it in the oven, watching it carefully after a few minutes, until it is completely crisp (it should be cracker consistency throughout without being burnt), about 2–3 minutes per side. Note: It can go from crisp to burnt pretty quickly so be sure to watch closely.

3 Spread ¼ cup of the ranch evenly over the lavash, leaving about a ½ inch outer perimeter of the lavash bare, as if you're spreading sauce over a pizza. Add the tomato slices side by side over the ranch. Then sprinkle the garlic evenly over them.

4 Bake the pizza until the ranch is hot and the tomatoes are cooked, about 5–8 minutes, making sure that the outer edges aren't burning (you can wrap foil around them if they are).

5 Meanwhile, place the bacon strips in a small nonstick frying pan. Cook them until the strips are crispy, but not burnt. Transfer them to a paper towel–lined plate to remove excess grease. Cut them into tiny slivers.

6 Remove the pizza from the oven. Top it evenly with the grilled chicken, chives, then bacon. Drizzle the remaining 2 tablespoons of the ranch over top. Cut the pizza into 12 equal pieces. Enjoy immediately.

CHOICES/EXCHANGES
1 ½ starch, 3 lean protein

PER SERVING
250 calories, 7 g fat, 1.5 g saturated fat, 0 g trans fat, 60 mg cholesterol, 400 mg sodium, 370 mg potassium, 19 g carbohydrate, 2 g fiber, 4 g sugars, 27 g protein, 185 mg phosphorus

THAI SHRIMP FLATBREAD PIZZA

Thai Shrimp Flatbread Pizza

If you're not familiar with it, lavash (aka Armenian lavash) is a flatbread that is said to have originated in Armenia, though some argue it originated in the Middle East. I love whole wheat lavash because you can make super light wraps, pizzas, and so much more from it. Just be careful—some brands now offered in the U.S. are not exactly as healthy as many of the traditional varieties. So with lavash, and all products, explore the labels of all brands the very first time you purchase it instead of just grabbing one.

Look for lavash or flatbread with no more than 150 calories and no more than 100 mg of sodium per 8 × 10 inch sheet.

8 ounces peeled and deveined extra large (about 21–25 count) shrimp (preferably wild caught)

½ teaspoon olive oil

1 teaspoon salt free Szechuan seasoning

1 piece (8 × 10 inch) whole wheat lavash or flatbread

¼ cup plus 2 tablespoons Peanut Satay Sauce (see page 189), divided

½ cup carrot matchsticks

½ cup cucumber matchsticks (seed the unpeeled cucumbers before cutting into matchsticks)

¼ cup green onion slivers (cut on an extreme diagonal)

*If you have the Peanut Satay Sauce prepared.

1 Preheat a grill to high.

2 Preheat the oven to 400°F. Line a baking sheet (large enough to fit the flatbread so that it lays flat) with nonstick foil.

3 In a medium bowl, toss the shrimp in the olive oil and the seasoning. Grill the shrimp until just barely translucent throughout (keep in mind that they will cook a tiny bit more in the oven, so you really don't want to overcook them).

4 Place the flatbread on the prepared baking sheet. Crisp it in the oven, watching it carefully after a few minutes, until it is completely crisp (it should be a cracker consistency throughout without being burnt), about 2–3 minutes per side. Note: This can go from crisp to burnt pretty quickly so be sure to watch closely after 2 minutes on each side.

5 Spread ¼ cup of the satay sauce evenly over the lavash, leaving about a ½ inch outer perimeter of the lavash bare, as if you're spreading sauce over a pizza.

6 Add the shrimp side by side evenly spaced over the sauce, preferably pointing them in the same direction (to look more restaurant quality). Bake the pizza until the sauce is hot, about 2–3 minutes, making sure that the outer edges aren't burning (you can wrap foil around the edges if they start to burn).

recipe continued on next page »

7 Remove the pizza from the oven. Top it evenly with the carrots, cucumber, and then the green onions. Drizzle the remaining 2 tablespoons sauce over top. Cut the pizza into 12 equal pieces. Enjoy immediately.

Cook's Notes

When crisping the lavash for a flatbread pizza, make sure that it is crisped even in the center. It should be as hard as a cracker. If it's not, the finished pizza will be soggy. Look for lavash with no more than 150 calories and no more than 100 mg of sodium per 8 × 10 inch sheet. I buy my favorite variety at my local grocery store, but it's a bit less pricey when I go to ethnic markets (Armenian, Persian, or other Middle Eastern markets often carry it if you happen to have one near you)! Want to know what variety I'm using? Visit me at **www.devinalexander.com/diabetes** and I'll show you!

It's super important to seed the cucumber in this recipe before cutting it into matchsticks. If you don't, they could make your pizza soggy. Visit me at **www.devinalexander.com/diabetes** to see what products and equipment I'm using, learn how to seed cucumbers, and so much more!

I'm all about making meals at home that look restaurant quality. To achieve that here, cut the green onions on an extreme diagonal—they'll look extra pretty! And use a mandolin that makes julienne cuts to create the matchstick carrots and cucumbers in seconds.

Once you top this pizza with the veggies, make sure you're enjoying it immediately or it could get soggy. When I serve this pizza at my Girls Night Thin™ Parties, I serve the veggies and the extra sauce on the side and have everyone top their own pizzas. It's fun and social and ensures a better end result.

CHOICES/EXCHANGES
1 ½ starch, 1 nonstarchy vegetables, 4 lean protein, 1 fat

PER SERVING
350 calories, 13 g fat, 2 g saturated fat, 0 g trans fat, 175 mg cholesterol, 440 mg sodium, 410 mg potassium, 26 g carbohydrate, 4 g fiber, 5 g sugars, 31 g protein, 260 mg phosphorus

Seared Wild Mushroom Toast

This sandwich is a spin on the popular "tartines" (or toasts) that are often found in trendy restaurants these days. Use a mix of mushrooms, if possible, for texture and variety in taste; though this recipe tastes great with any wild mushrooms.

2 teaspoons olive oil

8 ounces wild mushrooms (enoki, wood ear, baby cremini—it's best to use a mix), thinly sliced

¼ cup white wine

2 teaspoons chopped Roasted Garlic (see page 195)

¾ teaspoon fresh thyme leaves

1/16 teaspoon sea salt

1/16 teaspoon reduced sodium salt substitute

½ teaspoon flat leaf parsley leaves

Freshly ground black pepper, to taste

2 slices sprouted grain bread (no more than 80 calories per slice)

2 (¾ ounce) spreadable light Swiss cheese wedges

*If you have the Roasted Garlic prepared.

1 Place a large nonstick frying pan over high heat. When hot, add the oil. Add the mushrooms in a single layer. (If you don't have a pan large enough to do so, work in batches, using only the proportionate amount of oil per batch. The goal is to get a nice browning on the mushrooms, not to steam them, so they need to be in a single layer). Cook the mushrooms until the edges are browned and caramelized, about 2–3 minutes. Then flip them and brown the other side about 2–3 minutes.

2 Add the wine. Turn the heat to low and continue cooking the mushrooms until the wine is absorbed or reduced. Stir in the roasted garlic, thyme, salt, and salt substitute. Then, just before serving, stir in the parsley. Season with pepper.

3 Meanwhile, toast the bread until it is a light golden brown. On a serving plate or 2 dinner plates, spread one cheese wedge evenly over each slice of bread. Top each slice with half of the mushroom mixture. Enjoy immediately.

CHOICES/EXCHANGES
1 starch, 2 nonstarchy vegetable, 1 lean protein, 1 fat

PER SERVING
210 calories, 7 g fat, 1.7 g saturated fat, 0 g trans fat, 5 mg cholesterol, 390 mg sodium, 580 mg potassium, 27 g carbohydrate, 6 g fiber, 1 g sugars, 9 g protein, 315 mg phosphorus

PERFECT Party Fare & SAVORY Snacks

CRAB STUFFED SHRIMP

Crab Stuffed Shrimp

I love this appetizer! It's so easy and definitely wow worthy! I first ran a version of this recipe in a holiday seafood article I wrote for Muscle & Fitness *magazine. I got such a great response and found myself making it so many times, that I wanted to share it here in a version that not only body builders can enjoy.*

Don't know how to butterfly shrimp? It sounds fancier and more difficult than it is. Visit me at **www.devinalexander.com/ diabetes** *and I will show you how it's done.*

4 ounces drained, canned lump crab meat

2 tablespoons very finely chopped whole green onion

1 tablespoon light mayonnaise (preferably natural)

2 teaspoons lemon zest

1 teaspoon very finely chopped Fresno pepper

1 ½ tablespoons whole wheat panko (Japanese bread crumbs)

12 extra large (about 21–25 count) shrimp (preferably wild caught)

Olive oil spray (propellant free)

1 Preheat the oven to 475°F. Line a small baking sheet with nonstick foil.

2 Mix the crab, green onions, mayonnaise, lemon zest, and peppers in small bowl until they are well combined.

3 Spread the bread crumbs on a small plate and set aside.

4 To butterfly the shrimp: Peel all but the tail and last joint of the shell off the shrimp. On a cutting board, place a shrimp so that the head end and tail are touching the cutting board and the center arches toward the ceiling. Insert a knife into the shrimp near the head, just past the remaining shell, and cut down the center of the shrimp's back to the tail, cutting just deep enough to flatten the shrimp (make sure not to cut all the way through). Run the shrimp under cold water to clean it. Dry it well with paper towels. Repeat the procedure with the remaining shrimp and place them side by side, not touching, on the prepared baking sheet.

5 Divide the crab mixture evenly among the shrimp, about ½ tablespoon per shrimp, forming it into a tight mound on top of the butterflied portion of each shrimp.

recipe continued on next page »

6 Carefully dip each shrimp, gently turning it upside down, into the bread crumbs to lightly coat the crab (not the whole shrimp, just the portion with the crab). Return shrimp to the baking sheet and make sure the crab mound isn't flattened (if it is, reshape it slightly to look like a mound). Sprinkle any remaining bread crumbs evenly over the tops. Mist the tops lightly with spray.

7 Bake the shrimp 7–10 minutes or until they are no longer translucent throughout. Enjoy immediately.

Cook's Notes

If you don't have a zester, you can use a peeler to very lightly remove just the very outer layer of the lemon peel—don't go deep enough to include the pith (the white part of the peel). Then chop the peel extremely finely. Note that if you are using a zester, some zesters will give you thicker, almost ribbon like pieces of peel, while others yield fine shreds. For this recipe, it's much better to have fine shreds. If yours yields thicker pieces, it's best to chop the zest so it can be very well incorporated in each bite.

When handling any hot peppers, always be sure to wash your hands when you finish. The peppers will not burn your hands, but if you touch your eyes, it could be painful.

Panko, or Japanese bread crumbs, can be found in the international aisle at your grocery store, or with the other bread crumbs. Gluten free panko can be used instead of whole wheat panko to keep these yummy morsels gluten free, but be sure the panko variety you select isn't full of sodium. The whole wheat panko I use in this recipe has only 23 mg of sodium per ¼ cup, but a gluten free version that is made by the same company contains a whopping 380 mg of sodium per ¼ cup!

CHOICES/EXCHANGES
2 lean protein

PER SERVING
80 calories, 1.5 g fat, 0.3 g saturated fat, 0 g trans fat, 110 mg cholesterol, 220 mg sodium, 260 mg potassium, 3 g carbohydrate, 0 g fiber, 0 g sugars, 14 g protein, 190 mg phosphorus

Salmon Cucumber Party Bites

6 ounces skinless salmon fillet (preferably wild caught)

¾ teaspoon salt free garlic and herb bread seasoning

⅛ teaspoon sea salt

Olive oil spray (propellant free)

1 medium English cucumber

6 tablespoons Garlicky Dill Dip & Sauce (see page 181)

Fresh dill, for garnish

*If you have the Garlicky Dill Dip & Sauce prepared.

Cook's Notes

I recommend you purchase more than 6 ounces of salmon if you're making this recipe for a party and want the salmon pieces to be uniform. Always buy the thick end of salmon fillets. The tail end is tougher; the tail whips around as the fish swims creating a tougher cut of meat. When cutting the cubes, try to cut all of the cubes from the thick portion of the salmon for uniform pieces. Save the thinner portions for another recipe or fold a long, thin strip of the salmon over so that it resembles the cubes for even cooking.

1 Preheat the oven to 300°F. Line a small baking sheet with nonstick foil.

2 Cut the salmon into 12 equal sized cubes. Transfer them to a small bowl and sprinkle the seasoning and salt over them. Place them side by side, with the side that had the skin facing down, on the prepared baking sheet so they do not touch. Lightly mist them with spray. Bake them until they are cooked to the desired doneness, or just barely translucent in the center, about 4–6 minutes.

3 Meanwhile, run the tines of a fork from one end of the cucumber to the other in a straight line, tearing into the skin slightly to score it (when it's cut you'll have a cool pattern; visit **www.devinalexander.com/diabetes** for a video demonstration). Rotate the cucumber and repeat running the fork from one end of the cucumber to the other, starting with the fork close enough to the first set of score marks to continue the pattern. Repeat this all of the way around the cucumber. Cut the end from the cucumber on a slight diagonal and discard it. Next, cut 12 (¼ inch thick) cucumber slices on a slight diagonal (to yield about 6 ounces of cucumber slices total). Reserve the remaining cucumber for another recipe.

4 Place the cucumber slices side by side on a serving platter. Add ½ tablespoon of the Garlicky Dill Dip & Sauce to the center of each slice. Place one piece of salmon on each. Garnish with dill sprigs or freshly chopped dill leaves to taste, if desired. Enjoy immediately.

CHOICES/EXCHANGES
1 lean protein, 1 fat

PER SERVING
110 calories, 6 g fat, 1 g saturated fat, 0 g trans fat, 25 mg cholesterol, 150 mg sodium, 225 mg potassium, 2 g carbohydrate, 0 g fiber, 1 g sugars, 10 g protein, 110 mg phosphorus

Waffle Fry BBQ Bites

12 (about 4 ½ ounces) sweet potato waffle fries (preferably natural)

12 tablespoons BBQ Beef (see steps 1, 2, and 4 on page 22), reheated if necessary

1 ½ tablespoons barbecue sauce (look for one that's relatively low in sugar)

*If you have the BBQ Beef prepared.

1 Cook the fries according to package directions.

2 Transfer the cooked fries, evenly spaced, onto a serving platter in a single layer. Mound the beef evenly among them (about 1 tablespoon on each fry). Drizzle the sauce evenly over them.

Cook's Notes

Ideally, you'll have **12** relatively uniform pieces of fries for this recipe. If you don't and you're entertaining with them, cut 12 pieces to a uniform weight of about ⅓ ounce each before you bake them. If you are not entertaining, measure out 4 ½ ounces of fries, divide the beef proportionally among the fries, and eat one fourth of the fries, beef, and the sauce per serving. Want to save even more fat and calories? Consider making the fries yourself. Visit me at **www.devinalexander.com/diabetes** and I'll show you how! Plus, I'll share tons of chef secrets, tips, and tricks.

Try to find a barbecue sauce that has no more than **6–8 g of sugar per 2** tablespoon serving. A professional would use a squirt bottle to make the drizzle of barbecue sauce look perfect on this dish. If you don't have one, don't worry! You can add the sauce to a resealable plastic bag (toward one of the sealed corners). Cut the very tip of that corner off, and voilá—you, too, can create a perfect drizzle. Note that this technique is a bit easier if you use a bag that is a bit thicker, like a freezer bag; really thin bags are a bit tougher to wrangle.

CHOICES/EXCHANGES
½ starch, ½ carbohydrate, 1 lean protein

PER SERVING
120 calories, 4 g fat, 0.9 g saturated fat, 0 g trans fat, 20 mg cholesterol, 200 mg sodium, 200 mg potassium, 11 g carbohydrate, 1 g fiber, 4 g sugars, 10 g protein, 75 mg phosphorus

WAFFLE FRY BBQ BITES

Party Wontons

Asian food is notorious for being high in fat, saturated fat, calories, and sodium—at least the way we prepare it in the U.S. But it's so delicious I don't want to stay away from it! Fortunately, this recipe is one way I don't have to! Not only will you love these wontons, but your party guests will enjoy them too.

If you're not serving all of the wontons immediately, only bake as many as you're planning to enjoy right afterward. You can store the remainder of the filling in the refrigerator in an airtight plastic container for up to 3 days. Fill the wontons just prior to baking them.

2 tablespoons drained, sliced canned water chestnuts

1 medium carrot, peeled, trimmed, and each cut into 6 equal pieces

2 whole green onions, trimmed and each cut into thirds

1 medium clove garlic, peeled and ends trimmed

12 ounces 99% lean ground chicken breast (preferably free range)

¼ cup finely minced sweet onion

½ tablespoon sake or cooking sherry

2 teaspoons toasted or roasted sesame oil

1 ½ teaspoons freshly minced ginger

¼ teaspoon kosher salt

¼ teaspoon freshly ground black pepper

36 wonton wrappers (3 × 3 ½ inches each; preferably natural)

Olive oil spray (propellant free)

¼ cup prepared Chinese hot mustard for dipping

1 Preheat the oven to 400°F. Line a large baking sheet (or sheets) with nonstick foil.

2 Add the water chestnuts, carrots, green onion, and garlic to the bowl of a food processor fitted with a chopping blade. Process them until the ingredients are minced, scraping down the sides of the bowl if necessary. Add the chopped vegetables to a fine mesh strainer. Using a rubber spatula or a spoon, press out any moisture from the chopped veggies.

3 Add the vegetable mixture, ground chicken, onion, sake, sesame oil, ginger, salt, and pepper to a large glass or plastic mixing bowl. With a fork or clean hands, mix the ingredients until well combined.

4 Fill a small bowl with water. Place a wonton wrapper on a clean, flat work surface. Spoon about 1 tablespoon of the filling onto the center of the wrapper (use a 1 ¼ inch diameter cookie or meatball scoop for ease if you have one). Dip your finger into the water and run your fingertip along two adjacent edges of the wrapper. Fold the wrapper in half diagonally, creating a triangle. Gently press your finger around the edges of the wrapper, sealing the dry side to the moistened side, being careful not to leave any air bubbles. Press on the filling slightly to spread it out (if the mound of filling in the center is too thick, the wontons won't cook evenly). Transfer the wonton to the prepared baking sheet. Continue filling and sealing the remaining wonton wrappers, working in batches, if necessary, so that they all lay flat on the baking sheet(s) and are not touching.

5 Lightly mist the tops of the wontons with spray and bake them for 5 minutes (if you are using multiple baking sheets, be sure not to place the baking sheets on top of each other in the oven; placing them side by side or cooking one after the other is recommended to ensure more even cooking and "crisping"). Then gently flip the wontons, spray the tops with spray, and bake an additional 2–4 minutes, or until the outsides are lightly browned and the chicken is no longer pink.

6 Serve immediately with Chinese hot mustard for dipping, if desired.

Cook's Notes

If you have trouble finding extra lean ground chicken at your grocery store, don't worry. You can ask your butcher to grind chicken breasts for you. If they can't, it's easy to grind them yourself in your food processor. I'll show you how! Just visit me at **www.devinalexander.com/diabetes** to see a video...and so much more!

Look for wonton wrappers with as little sodium as possible.

You can find Chinese hot mustard in the Asian food aisle of your grocery store.

CHOICES/EXCHANGES
½ starch, 1 nonstarchy vegetable, 1 lean protein

PER SERVING
90 calories, 2 g fat, 0 g saturated fat, 0 g trans fat, 15 mg cholesterol, 150 mg sodium, 95 mg potassium, 12 g carbohydrate, 1 g fiber, 1 g sugars, 7 g protein, 50 mg phosphorus

Lean & Loaded Nachos

People are always surprised to learn that I eat nachos, especially knowing that I've kept 70 pounds off for 30 years. But the nachos I eat (these Lean & Loaded ones included) are actually a balanced meal with a whopping 36 g of protein, 36 g of complex carbohydrates, and 5 g of fiber. I sometimes add greens to the top too! Either way, they're delicious and won't add to your waistline.

4 ounces 99% lean ground turkey

1 teaspoon salt free Mexican or Southwest seasoning

⅛ teaspoon reduced sodium salt substitute

Olive oil spray (propellant free)

1 ounce lightly salted baked tortilla chips

2 ½ tablespoons no salt added canned black beans, rinsed, drained well, and heated

¼ cup finely chopped seeded tomato

2 ½ tablespoons salsa con queso or nacho cheese sauce (preferably natural and no more than 3 g fat per 2 tablespoon serving), heated

2 tablespoons very thinly sliced jalapeño (rounds)

1–2 tablespoons coarsely chopped cilantro leaves, or to taste

1 In a small bowl, using a fork, mix the turkey, seasoning, and salt substitute until well combined.

2 Place a small nonstick frying pan over medium heat. When hot, mist it with spray. Add the turkey and cook, breaking it into chunks as you do (don't crumble it into tiny pieces, you want it to be chunky and yummy!) until it is cooked through.

3 Place the chips in a single layer, evenly covering a dinner plate. Top them evenly with the beans, tomatoes, then the turkey. Drizzle the cheese sauce evenly over the top. Top with the jalapeño and cilantro. Enjoy immediately.

Cook's Notes

Look for salted baked tortilla chips with no more than 4.5 g of fat and 50 mg of sodium per serving.

Don't know how to seed a tomato? Visit me at **www.devinalexander.com/diabetes** where I show you how to do it easily in a video!

Always wash your hands after touching jalapeños or wear rubber gloves when handling these peppers. They won't burn your hands, but if the oils remain on your hands and you touch your eyes, it could be painful.

CHOICES/EXCHANGES
2 starch, 1 nonstarchy vegetable, 4 lean protein

PER SERVING
350 calories, 8 g fat, 3.5 g saturated fat, 0.1 g trans fat, 75 mg cholesterol, 330 mg sodium, 930 mg potassium, 36 g carbohydrate, 5 g fiber, 4 g sugars, 36 g protein, 465 mg phosphorus

LEAN & LOADED NACHOS

Seasoned Sweet Potato Chips

I love making these chips from light sweet potatoes. A lot of people don't realize it, but there are tons of varieties of sweet potatoes. Orange ones, purple ones, and those that are cream colored with light brown skins. I love the light fleshed variety because they taste most similar to white potatoes, but have nutrients very similar to the orange sweet potatoes. If you have a loved one who thinks they don't like sweet potatoes, you might just convert them with these!

Note that these chips taste better if they are a little overcooked than undercooked (when undercooked, they are chewy and not chip like). So don't pull them out of the oven too early.

*I use a small hand held mandolin to slice my chips. This tool is a great investment, especially if you get one with a lot of attachments. Don't know how to choose one? Don't worry. I'll show you! Visit me at **www.devinalexander.com/diabetes** and you'll find info about my favorite mandolin and so much more!*

1 large (about 12 ounces) light fleshed sweet potato, peeled

2 ½ teaspoons olive oil

1 teaspoon 33% less sodium crab boil seasoning

1 Preheat the oven to 300°F. Line 3 large baking sheets with nonstick foil (or work in batches if necessary).

2 Slice the potato into nearly paper thin rounds (use a mandolin or a slicing blade of a food processor for consistency and ease if you have either). Transfer the potato slices to a large resealable plastic bag and drizzle the oil over them. Sprinkle them with the seasoning. Toss the potatoes in the bag to evenly coat them.

3 Arrange the potatoes in a single layer on the prepared baking sheets. Bake them for 15 minutes. Then flip them and continue cooking them until they are completely crisp throughout (they're delicious when they're crisped completely, not chewy). After about 8 minutes, begin watching them very closely—you'll want to remove any potatoes that cook faster and are completely crisp (be careful not to burn them). Cook them on the second side for up to another 15 minutes, depending on the size of the potato slices.

4 Remove them from the oven and allow them to cool for about 5 minutes. Enjoy immediately.

CHOICES/EXCHANGES
1 starch, ½ fat

PER SERVING
90 calories, 3 g fat, 0 g saturated fat, 0 g trans fat, 0 mg cholesterol, 135 mg sodium, 240 mg potassium, 14 g carbohydrate, 2 g fiber, 3 g sugars, 1 g protein, 35 mg phosphorus

Snickerdoodle Kettlecorn

This recipe should make about 4–5 cups of popped corn. If kernels are left unpopped, you should still be consuming about 50 calories per popped cup.

It's super important that you season the popcorn immediately after it comes off the heat or else the cinnamon, sugar, and salt won't stick.

2 teaspoons stevia brown sugar blend (such as Truvia Brown Sugar Blend)

¼ teaspoon ground cinnamon

¼ teaspoon sea salt

½ tablespoon vegan butter (from a stick, not a tub)

¼ cup unpopped yellow corn kernels

1 In a small bowl, mix the brown sugar blend, cinnamon, and salt.

2 Heat a large nonstick pot over high heat. When just hot, add the butter and the kernels. Place a lid on the pot so that it's not quite closed. Shake the pot every 30 seconds to redistribute the kernels, allowing them to pop until the popping slows to about 5 seconds between pops.

3 Remove the popcorn from the heat and immediately sprinkle the cinnamon mixture over top. Using two rubber spatulas, gently toss the popped corn until evenly coated. Transfer the popcorn to a large bowl or 4 smaller serving bowls. Enjoy immediately or allow it to cool and store it in an airtight container for up to 2 days.

CHOICES/EXCHANGES
½ starch, ½ fat

PER SERVING
60 calories, 2 g fat, 1 g saturated fat, 0 g trans fat, 0 mg cholesterol, 140 mg sodium, 35 mg potassium, 10 g carbohydrate, 2 g fiber, 1 g sugars, 1 g protein, 25 mg phosphorus

BRUSSELS SALMON "SLIDERS"

Brussels Salmon "Sliders"

I love salmon, but I think it is one of the worst foods on the planet when it is overcooked! Please please please do not overcook your salmon!

Many years ago, I was doing a show for Noggin Network. We were helping teens lose weight. I was doing on camera demos of the kids' favorite comfort foods, and another chef was preparing their daily meals. After realizing that the crew was eating pizza and super fattening foods, I asked to eat with the kids. Imagine my absolute horror when I realized the kids had never previously even tried salmon (or any fish) and the cook was ruining it—it was so dry and fishy that I had to (carefully) intervene and talk to the producers!

While it's true that the purpose of TV shows is to get a great story, behind the scenes, I can't help but care about the "characters" as people, not characters. The difference between well cooked salmon and well sourced veggies over dry salmon and canned veggies could make or break someone's interest in healthy food! If I could only eat that cook's salmon or veggies from a can, I, too, would be sneaking a lot more unhealthy foods.

12 small pieces Brussels sprouts (about 12 ounces)

½ tablespoon extra virgin olive oil

½ teaspoon plus ¼ teaspoon salt free garlic and herb bread seasoning, divided

⅛ teaspoon sea salt

⅛ teaspoon reduced sodium salt substitute

¼ teaspoon freshly ground black pepper, or to taste

6 ounces skinless salmon fillet (preferably wild caught)

Olive oil spray (propellant free)

2 tablespoons Dijon mustard

12 decorative toothpicks

1 Preheat the oven to 400°F. Line a medium baking sheet with nonstick foil.

2 Trim the ends of the Brussels sprouts and remove any tough or yellow outer leaves. Cut the sprouts in half across the stems. Transfer them to a small mixing bowl. Drizzle the olive oil over top. Then sprinkle with ½ teaspoon of the seasoning, the salt, salt substitute, and pepper and toss them until the ingredients are well combined. Spread the sprouts on the prepared baking sheets in a single layer. Bake them for 10 minutes, then, using a spatula, flip them. Continue baking them until the sprouts are lightly browned and crisped in spots, about an additional 5–9 minutes.

3 Meanwhile, cut the salmon into 12 even pieces (about ½ ounce each), making sure that if any of the brown on the bottom of the fillet exists, it is trimmed off completely. Transfer them to a small bowl and gently toss the pieces in the remaining ¼ teaspoon seasoning until evenly coated.

recipe continued on next page »

4 Place a large nonstick frying pan over medium high heat. When hot, remove it from the heat just long enough to mist it with spray. Add the salmon pieces to the pan so they do not touch, working in batches, if necessary, and misting the pan between batches. When the salmon is a light golden brown on the bottom, about 30 seconds to 1 minute, flip it and lightly brown the other side. If it's not cooked through to your liking, turn the heat to low and continue cooking it until it is (these pieces will cook fast, so watch closely).

5 Place one Brussels sprout half, cut side up, on a plate. Top it with a piece of salmon. Add ½ teaspoon mustard to the inside of a second sprout half. Use it to top the salmon, creating a "slider" and secure the "slider" with a toothpick that is inserted perpendicular to the plate from the top to the bottom of the slider. Repeat with the remaining sprouts, salmon, and mustard.

Cook's Notes

When selecting salmon for this recipe, buy a fillet that is an even thickness and cut from the thicker end of the fillet (the tail end can be really tough and is generally very thin). If you want your "sliders" to look perfectly uniformed, buy a bigger piece and use the extra for another recipe.

CHOICES/EXCHANGES
1 nonstarchy vegetable, 1 lean protein, ½ fat

PER SERVING
100 calories, 4 g fat, 1 g saturated fat, 0 g trans fat, 25 mg cholesterol, 220 mg sodium, 490 mg potassium, 6 g carbohydrate, 3 g fiber, 1 g sugars, 11 g protein, 125 mg phosphorus

Open-Face Bacon Cheese "Sliders"

I first developed a version of this recipe for a burger article I wrote for Men's Fitness *magazine. It was such a crowd pleaser among low carb and gluten free eaters, I thought it was the perfect fit to redevelop as party fare for this diabetes friendly book!*

4 medium plum or Roma tomatoes, cut in half through the stem and seeded

8 ounces 96% lean ground beef (preferably grass fed)

2 teaspoons dried minced onion

⅛ teaspoon kosher salt

Freshly ground black pepper, to taste

1 ½ ounces extra light sharp cheddar cheese slivers (preferably natural)

½ cup red onion slivers, or to taste

2 slices center cut bacon (preferably natural and nitrate free), cut into quarters

1 Preheat the broiler. Line a small baking sheet with nonstick foil.

2 Place the tomatoes, not touching, on the prepared baking sheet.

3 In a bowl, mix the ground beef, onion, salt, and pepper until well combined. Divide the mixture equally among the tomatoes, filling them and flattening the overflowing meat on top to look like burger patties on a bun. After the beef is in place, use your index finger to create a slight divot in the center; this will help keep them balanced and standing upright (if you're serving them for guests, consider creating "bumpers" from pieces of foil to ensure they stay upright while cooking).

4 Top each equally with the cheese. Divide the onions evenly over them and then add ¼ strip of bacon over top of each.

5 Broil them until the bacon is cooked, tomatoes are warm, and the beef is cooked to desired doneness, about 4–7 minutes. Enjoy immediately.

Cook's Notes

Don't know how to seed a tomato? Visit me at **www.devinalexander.com/ diabetes** where I show you how to do it easily in a video!

CHOICES/EXCHANGES
1 nonstarchy vegetable, 2 lean protein, 1 fat

PER SERVING
160 calories, 8 g fat, 3.1 g saturated fat, 0.2 g trans fat, 40 mg cholesterol, 260 mg sodium, 400 mg potassium, 5 g carbohydrate, 1 g fiber, 3 g sugars, 18 g protein, 200 mg phosphorus

SHRIMP GUAC APPS

Shrimp Guac Apps

I serve these crazy, yummy, insanely easy morsels at my Girls Night Thin™ parties all the time. They are truly one of my favorite in-a-hurry appetizers and they're always a huge hit! They come together in minutes and look so elegant that people often comment that I "must have spent so much time on them"!

12 large (36–40 count) shrimp (preferably wild caught)

1 teaspoon olive oil

½ teaspoon salt free Mexican or southwest seasoning

1/16 teaspoon sea salt

1 medium English cucumber

6 tablespoons prepared guacamole

Cook's Notes

Look for a prepared guacamole that is natural and as light as possible. Compare labels and try to select a light option without a lot of sodium.

1 Preheat a grill to high.

2 Peel all but the tail and last joint of the shell off the shrimp and devein them by cutting a slit down the back and then running them under cold water. Dry them well with paper towels. Add the shrimp to a small bowl and toss them in the olive oil, seasoning, and salt. Place them side by side on the grill so they do not touch. Grill them until they are no longer translucent, about 1 minute per side.

3 Meanwhile, run the tines of a fork from one end of the cucumber to the other in a straight line, tearing into the skin slightly to score it (when it's cut you'll have a cool pattern; visit **www.devinalexander.com/diabetes** for a video demonstration). Rotate the cucumber and repeat running the fork down the length of the cucumber, starting with the fork close enough to the first set of score marks to continue the pattern. Repeat this all the way around the cucumber. Cut the end from the cucumber on a slight diagonal and discard it. Then, cut 12 (about ¼ inch thick, not thicker) cucumber slices on a slight diagonal (to yield about 6 ounces of cucumber slices total). Reserve any remaining cucumber for another recipe.

4 Place the cucumber slices side by side on a serving platter. Add ½ tablespoon of the guacamole to the center of each slice. Place one shrimp on each so that it's standing up with the tail nearly at the top. Enjoy immediately.

CHOICES/EXCHANGES
1 nonstarchy vegetable, 1 lean protein, ½ fat

PER SERVING
90 calories, 4 g fat, 0.5 g saturated fat, 0 g trans fat, 65 mg cholesterol, 160 mg sodium, 150 mg potassium, 4 g carbohydrate, 2 g fiber, 1 g sugars, 10 g protein, 95 mg phosphorus

SIX PACK
Salads

Shrimp, Orange & Avocado Salad

4 ounces extra large (about 21–25 count) peeled and deveined shrimp (preferably wild caught)

¼ teaspoon salt free garlic and herb bread seasoning

½ teaspoon plus 1 teaspoon extra virgin olive oil, divided

2 teaspoons freshly squeezed lime juice

1 teaspoon freshly minced garlic

1 medium, seedless orange

4 cups loosely packed spinach leaves, washed and dried very well, coarse stems removed

¼ ripe medium avocado, cut into ¼ inch pieces (about ¼ cup)

1 tablespoon finely chopped red onion

1 tablespoon dry roasted pepitas (pumpkin seeds)

½ ounce (about 1 ½ tablespoons) crumbled part skim queso fresco

Freshly ground black pepper, to taste, if desired

Cook's Notes

If you're not familiar with queso fresco, I liken it to the Mexican version of the Greek feta cheese. Like feta, it's sold in a block (usually a round block in the case of queso fresco) and it can be crumbled.

1 Preheat a grill to high.

2 In a small mixing bowl, toss the shrimp in the seasoning and ½ teaspoon olive oil. Set aside.

3 In a small bowl or ramekin, mix the lime juice, the remaining 1 teaspoon olive oil, and the garlic. Set aside

4 Cut a slice off both ends of the orange just thick enough to cut off the peel and pith (the white part). Place the orange on a flat surface. Carefully following the natural curve of the orange, cut away the peel and pith in strips using a small paring knife, beginning at the top and ending at the bottom (try not to cut away the flesh of the orange). Continue peeling until all the peel and pith are removed. Then, carefully cut between the "skins" of the orange to remove the orange sections, trying to keep them as whole as possible as you do (this is how you supreme an orange). Squeeze the remaining portion (the skins) of the orange over the bowl with the lime juice and olive oil to release any remaining juice into the bowl, then discard the skins.

5 Grill the shrimp until they are no longer translucent throughout, about 1–2 minutes per side.

6 To a large serving bowl, add the spinach, avocado, red onion, half of the orange sections (reserve the remaining half of the orange sections for snacking, or for another recipe), and half of the pepitas. Pour the lime juice mixture over top and toss the salad until well combined. Top the salad with the queso fresco, the remaining pepitas, and then the shrimp. Season with pepper. Enjoy immediately.

CHOICES/EXCHANGES
½ fruit, 2 nonstarchy vegetable, 4 lean protein, 2 ½ fat

PER SERVING
380 calories, 20 g fat, 4.4 g saturated fat, 0.1 g trans fat, 200 mg cholesterol, 320 mg sodium, 1360 mg potassium, 21 g carbohydrate, 8 g fiber, 9 g sugars, 34 g protein, 475 mg phosphorus

Tuscan Chopped Salad

I try to prep ingredients in the beginning of the week so I can easily throw meals together when life gets busier than expected. I often have grilled chicken (or salmon, which is also awesome on this salad!) and grilled or raw asparagus on hand. And I always keep the Rockin' Body Balsamic dressing (page 185) in a salad cruet in my refrigerator—it lasts for months in the refrigerator as long as you don't add any fresh herbs or fresh garlic (ingredients like olive oil and vinegar will last and last in the refrigerator!)—which allows me to throw this salad together in minutes.

4 cups arugula leaves, coarsely chopped

½ cup asparagus, chopped on a diagonal into 1 inch pieces

¼ cup roasted red peppers, cut into strips

¼ cup rehydrated sundried tomatoes, cut into slivers

2 large fresh basil leaves, stems removed and cut into thin slivers (aka basil chiffonade)

4 teaspoons Rockin' Body Balsamic (see page 185)

⅛ teaspoon sea salt

Freshly ground black pepper, to taste

4 ounces Have-On-Hand Grilled Chicken (see page 192) or other leftover, extra lean grilled chicken breast (preferably free range), cut into strips

*If you have the Rockin' Body Balsamic and Have-On-Hand Grilled Chicken prepared.

1 Add the arugula, asparagus, roasted red peppers, sundried tomatoes, and basil to a medium mixing bowl. Drizzle the dressing over top. Toss the salad. Season it with salt and pepper.

2 Top the salad with the chicken breast. Enjoy immediately.

Cook's Notes

Asparagus can be eaten raw, though many people prefer it steamed or grilled. I much prefer the taste and texture of it raw or grilled over steamed.

Try roasting your own red peppers; the jarred varieties from the store are often full of sodium. See Roasted Red Peppers on page 196 for instructions on how to make your own.

When buying sundried tomatoes, be sure to check the labels. Obviously, you don't want to opt for those packed in oil, but even beyond that you might find some surprises. I found one package that had 25 mg of sodium per ½ ounce serving and another with a whopping 150 mg of sodium for the same serving size. If I hadn't read the nutritional information, I never would have realized the difference. Look for a variety without much added salt. Don't know how to rehydrate sundried tomatoes or chiffonade basil (aka cut it into slivers)? Or visit me at **www.devinalexander.com/diabetes** where I'll give you video demos and other chef secrets!

CHOICES/EXCHANGES
2 nonstarchy vegetable, 4 lean protein

PER SERVING
240 calories, 8 g fat, 1 g saturated fat, 0 g trans fat, 65 mg cholesterol, 290 mg sodium, 805 mg potassium, 11 g carbohydrate, 3 g fiber, 6 g sugars, 30 g protein, 305 mg phosphorus

Spinach Salad with Warm Bacon Dressing

This is a great salad to enjoy on special occasions. The flavors complement a Thanksgiving or holiday meal so well, and the salad adds to the elegance and indulgence of the day! Plus who doesn't want a bit of extra bacon yumminess on the Thanksgiving table? That being said, the dish is lean enough to enjoy more often than just holidays. And if you compare it to the traditional version of a spinach salad with bacon dressing, you might just be blown away.

3 cups loosely packed baby spinach leaves (course stems removed before measuring)

½ cup sliced button mushrooms

2 tablespoons Devinly Warm Bacon Dressing (see page 187), reheated if necessary

4 ounces Have-On-Hand Grilled Chicken (see page 192), sliced

*If you have the Devinly Warm Bacon Dressing and Have-On-Hand Grilled Chicken prepared.

1 Combine the spinach and mushrooms in a medium bowl. Add the dressing and toss until combined. Transfer the salad to a serving bowl or plate for a more elegant presentation. Top with the chicken. Enjoy immediately.

Cook's Notes

Make sure to peel or clean your mushrooms with a damp paper towel before using them. You never want to run mushrooms under water—they act like sponges and will hold on to water, which will dilute their yumminess. Don't know how to peel mushrooms? Don't worry. I'll show you. Visit **www.devinalexander.com/diabetes** for a video demo.

CHOICES/EXCHANGES
1 nonstarchy vegetable, 5 lean protein, ½ fat

PER SERVING
260 calories, 10 g fat, 2.8 g saturated fat, 0 g trans fat, 95 mg cholesterol, 410 mg sodium, 920 mg potassium, 6 g carbohydrate, 3 g fiber, 2 g sugars, 37 g protein, 335 mg phosphorus

SPINACH SALAD WITH WARM BACON DRESSING

Kale Grapefruit Pomegranate Salad

I threw this salad together one night when a friend stopped by using the limited ingredients in my fridge. And I was instantly hooked. It's so easy and so different. When pomegranates are in season, it's a must-try!

3 cups loosely packed, coarsely chopped fresh baby kale leaves

1–1 ½ tablespoons Champagne Vinaigrette (see page 186)

¾ ounce (about 3 tablespoons, not packed) crumbled light goat cheese (preferably natural), divided

2 tablespoons pomegranate arils (seeds), divided

¼ large (about 2 ounces) pink grapefruit, sectioned and peeled

4 ounces Have-On-Hand Grilled Chicken (see page 192), sliced

*If you have the Champagne Vinaigrette and Have-On-Hand Grilled Chicken prepared.

1 In a medium mixing bowl, toss the kale with 1 tablespoon of the vinaigrette, massaging it with clean hands for a minute. Add half the cheese and half of the pomegranate arils and toss the salad again. Taste the greens—I find 1 tablespoon of dressing to be enough; you might too. If not, add an additional ½ tablespoon and toss the salad again (or save the ½ tablespoon to dip the chicken in).

2 Mound the salad mixture on a plate. Arrange the grapefruit sections evenly around the edges of the salad. Sprinkle the remaining cheese and pomegranate arils over the top. Arrange the sliced chicken to one side of the salad. Enjoy immediately.

Cook's Notes

Though it is not going to harm you to eat any of the stems from the kale leaves, I highly recommend you remove them prior to chopping or measuring your kale. Stems poking into your mouth (obviously) take away from the restaurant quality feel of a dish, which I strive to achieve even at home on a regular basis.

Don't know how to easily section a grapefruit? Visit me at **www.devinalexander.com/diabetes** and I'll show you how!

CHOICES/EXCHANGES
½ fruit, 2 nonstarchy, 5 lean protein, 1 ½ fat

PER SERVING
360 calories, 14 g fat, 4.2 g saturated fat, 0 g trans fat, 100 mg cholesterol, 430 mg sodium, 760 mg potassium, 20 g carbohydrate, 5 g fiber, 10 g sugars, 39 g protein, 375 mg phosphorus

Asian Brown Rice Salad

1 cup uncooked short grain brown rice

2–4 tablespoons rice wine vinegar (aka rice vinegar), or to taste

½ tablespoon freshly minced ginger

1 ½ teaspoons roasted or toasted sesame oil

1 cup finely chopped whole green onion

¾ cup ¼ inch mango cubes

¾ cup red bell pepper matchsticks

½ cup very thinly sliced (on a diagonal) snap peas

½ teaspoon sea salt

1 Add 1 ½ cups of cold water to a medium saucepan (one with a lid). Add the rice. Place the pan over high heat and bring it to a boil. When the water boils, place a lid on the pan and reduce heat to low; simmer for 45–50 minutes or until all of the water is absorbed. Turn off the heat and let it stand for 10 minutes.

2 Meanwhile, add the vinegar and ginger to a small mixing bowl. Using a whisk, stir them until combined. Slowly whisk in the sesame oil. Set aside.

3 Place the cooled rice in a large bowl and add the green onion, mango, red bell pepper, and snap peas. Pour the vinegar mixture over the top and sprinkle with the salt. Toss the salad. Serve immediately or refrigerate in an airtight plastic or glass container for up to 1 day.

Cook's Notes

I love short grain brown rice over long or medium grain. It's a bit nuttier in flavor and has a slightly more al dente kind of texture. That said, some people prefer long grain, as it more mimics the texture of white rice. Use whatever variety you enjoy most! If you do opt for a grain other than short, follow the cooking instructions on the package, omitting any butter, oil, or salt.

Also note that brown rice is known to have relatively high levels of arsenic...even more so than white rice. So before you purchase brown rice, make sure you do research on the brand you're buying to make sure they're taking measures to keep arsenic levels as low as possible. Sound overwhelming? Don't worry! I have your back. Go to www.devinalexander.com/diabetes where I share my current picks for a variety of products and share chef cooking secrets including how to remove the strings from your snap peas to use them in this yummy rice salad!

To make the salad look restaurant quality, simply slice the snap peas on a diagonal. That's what I did in my restaurant, and it's a great tip for home cooks.

CHOICES/EXCHANGES
1 ½ starch, ½ carbohydrate

PER SERVING
160 calories, 2 g fat, 0 g saturated fat, 0 g trans fat, 0 mg cholesterol, 200 mg sodium, 205 mg potassium, 32 g carbohydrate, 3 g fiber, 5 g sugars, 3 g protein, 10 mg phosphorus

THAI LIME QUINOA SALAD

Thai Lime Quinoa Salad

Lime juice and lemon juice, when used right, can bring "magic" to so many dishes! The burst of virtually no calorie flavor when used in the right proportions is so refreshing and transformational. Just be sure that you don't cut corners and buy lime or lemon juice that is bottled. Trust me when I tell you, you always want to squeeze your lemon and lime juice from fresh lemons or limes! Even the stuff that says "100% lemon juice" doesn't taste as good as the juice from real lemons! If you're tempted to opt for the bottled stuff, try them side by side. You'll see what I mean!

2 cups cooked quinoa, chilled or warm

½ cup red bell pepper matchsticks

½ cup yellow bell pepper matchsticks

½ cup carrot matchsticks

¼ cup dry roasted unsalted peanut halves

¼ cup very thinly sliced (on a diagonal) whole green onions

3 tablespoons freshly squeezed lime juice

2 teaspoons extra virgin olive oil

¼ teaspoon plus ⅛ teaspoon sea salt

¼ cup coarsely chopped cilantro leaves

1 Toss the quinoa, red and yellow peppers, carrots, peanuts, and green onion together in a medium glass or plastic mixing bowl.

2 Pour the lime juice and olive oil over the quinoa mixture. Sprinkle in the salt and cilantro and toss the salad until the ingredients are well combined. Enjoy immediately or refrigerate in an airtight contain for up to 1 day.

Cook's Notes

I almost always use a julienne mandolin to cut my veggies into matchsticks. It saves an insane amount of time, even though I'm a chef and I'm quick with a knife. Have no idea what "julienne" or "mandolin" is? I'm here for you. Pop over to **www.devinalexander.com/diabetes** and I'll show you! I'll even give you tips on ordering one.

*If you have the quinoa prepared.

CHOICES/EXCHANGES
1 ½ starch, 2 fat

PER SERVING
210 calories, 9 g fat, 1 g saturated fat, 0 g trans fats, 0 mg cholesterol, 230 mg sodium, 355 mg potassium, 26 g carbohydrate, 5 g fiber, 3 g sugars, 7 g protein, 185 mg phosphorus

Mafia Quinoa Salad

I made a dish that was somewhat similar to this on camera for The Biggest Loser. The contestants loved it, and I got a lot of letters about it from fans saying it kind of tastes like an Italian sub! Since that time, I've switched from using wheat couscous to quinoa and made a few other tweaks to make it even cleaner. Now it can also be enjoyed by my gluten free diet following friends and fans—the more the merrier at Italian tables!

1 cup uncooked white or red quinoa

1 ½ cups (¼ inch dice) seeded Roma tomatoes

1 ½ cups (¼ inch dice) green bell pepper

¾ cup (¼ inch dice) red onion

¾ cup canned, drained, sliced black olives

⅓ cup (about 1 ½ ounces) drained and chopped pepperoncini slices, or to taste

1 tablespoon freshly minced garlic

1–2 tablespoons red wine vinegar, or more to taste

1 tablespoon extra virgin olive oil

1 teaspoon dried oregano leaves, or to taste, crumbled in your fingers if the leaves aren't pretty fine

¼ teaspoon sea salt

⅛ teaspoon crushed pepper flakes, or more to taste

1 In a fine sieve, rinse the quinoa under cold water. Shake off any excess water.

2 Add the quinoa and 1 cup of water to a medium saucepan with a lid. Bring the water to a boil. Reduce the heat to a simmer and cover the pan. Simmer it for 20–25 minutes or until all of the water is absorbed. Let it stand 5 minutes. Fluff the quinoa with a fork, then allow it to cool to room temperature.

3 Add the tomatoes, bell pepper, onion, olives, pepperoncini, and garlic to a large glass or plastic bowl. Toss them well to combine. Stir in the cooked quinoa until well combined. Stir in 1 tablespoon of the vinegar, and the olive oil. Season with oregano, salt, and pepper flakes. Then, taste it and add more vinegar, if desired (I like this salad with 2 tablespoons of vinegar, but in serving this recipe to guests, I've found that some people prefer it with more and others with less). Enjoy immediately or refrigerate in a resealable container for up to 2 days.

Cook's Notes

When making this salad, and all salads, it's so imperative (picture me jumping up and down, passionately begging you to heed this advice) to make sure your veggies, olives, and pepperoncini are all as dry as possible and that the quinoa is not wet! If you don't, you'll have a soggy salad instead of the restaurant quality one you can have if you execute the recipe as intended.

Don't know how to seed a tomato? Visit me at www.devinalexander.com/diabetes where I show you how to do it easily in a video!

CHOICES/EXCHANGES
1 starch, 1 fat

PER SERVING
130 calories, 4.5 g fat, 0.5 g saturated fat, 0 g trans fat, 0 mg cholesterol, 250 mg sodium, 280 mg potassium, 19 g carbohydrate, 3 g fiber, 2 g sugars, 4 g protein, 115 mg phosphorous

MAFIA QUINOA SALAD

Lemon Pistachio Quinoa Salad

At Devinly Decadence, my restaurants on Royal Caribbean Cruise line, we offered a buffet lunch of yummy, fresh, flavorful salads for a while. I served this salad and it was a huge hit—so much so that I was surprised. Granted, it tastes super fresh between the freshly squeezed lemon juice and the arugula. But I'm more of a "spicy gal". I tend to veer toward super bold flavors. That said, I love eating this salad and often top it with a piece of freshly grilled salmon to create an entire meal.

6 cups arugula, coarse stems removed, and torn

2 cups cooked quinoa

¼ cup shelled, dry roasted pistachios

¼ cup freshly squeezed lemon juice

2 teaspoons extra virgin olive oil

1 teaspoon finely minced fresh garlic

¼ teaspoon plus ⅛ teaspoon sea salt

1 Add the arugula, quinoa, pistachios, lemon juice, olive oil, garlic, and salt to a medium bowl.

2 Toss the salad until the ingredients are well combined. Enjoy immediately.

Cook's Notes

Throughout this book, I make it a point to write "freshly squeezed" and "freshly minced" for many of the ingredients. I wish I could come to your home, look you in the eyes, and tell you how very much it makes a difference, especially with a dish like this one! When additional ingredients are added to the juice or garlic (most commonly citric acid), they just don't have the same burst of fresh flavor, and the dish loses my Devinly seal of approval.

CHOICES/EXCHANGES
1 ½ starch, 1 nonstarchy vegetable, 1 ½ fat

PER SERVING
190 calories, 8 g fat, 1 g saturated fat, 0 g trans fat, 0 mg cholesterol, 230 mg sodium, 375 mg potassium, 25 g carbohydrate, 4 g fiber, 2 g sugars, 7 g protein, 195 mg phosphorus

N'Awlins Potato Salad

I was sent to New Orleans by Nightline back in 2010 to help a family who'd been struck by Hurricane Katrina. The super sweet Phillips family welcomed me into their home with open arms to help them and their grandchildren figure out how to grocery shop and cook given all the constraints they had to deal with. This potato salad was the result of an overhaul we did on the family's favorite potato salad recipe. They quickly embraced it, and I bet you will too!

2 ¼ pounds light fleshed sweet potatoes

¾ cup plain fat free quark or fat free Greek yogurt

1 tablespoon plus 2 teaspoons yellow mustard

½ tablespoon white vinegar

1 tablespoon plus 1 teaspoon extra virgin olive oil

⅔ cup finely chopped whole green onion

1 cup (¼ inch pieces) chopped celery

¼ cup finely chopped fresh parsley leaves

½ teaspoon plus ⅛ teaspoon sea salt

Freshly ground black pepper, to taste

1 Place a large pot of water over high heat. Bring the water to a boil.

2 Peel the potatoes and cut them into 1 inch pieces. When the water boils, carefully add the potatoes and boil them for 14–16 minutes or until very tender. Then drain them and bring them to room temperature.

3 Add the quark or yogurt, mustard, and vinegar to a small mixing bowl. Whisk the dressing together until it is well combined, then whisk in the olive oil. Stir in the green onion, celery, and parsley until combined.

4 Transfer the cooled potatoes to a large glass or plastic mixing bowl and pour the dressing over them. With a wooden spoon, mix the potatoes with the dressing, taking care to slightly mash some of the potatoes so that the salad is creamy. Season with salt and pepper.

5 Refrigerate for 1 hour, or up to 3 days, in an airtight plastic container. Enjoy.

Cook's Notes

When a recipe calls for green onions, it generally means that you should use both the green portion and white portion of the onion. If it says "green onion tops," that's when you just use the green part. There seems to be a lot of confusion about that.

CHOICES/EXCHANGES
1 ½ starch, ½ fat

PER SERVING
130 calories, 2.5 g fat, 0 g saturated fat, 0 g trans fat, 0 mg cholesterol, 250 mg sodium, 420 mg potassium, 24 g carbohydrate, 3 g fiber, 2 g sugars, 4 g protein, 50 mg phosphorus

CHICKEN PINWHEELS WITH SUNDRIED TOMATOES & GOAT CHEESE · 106

Japanese London Broil

¼ sheet (about 0.75 grams) toasted nori (seaweed)

1 dried (about 1.1 grams) Japones chili pepper

Finely grated zest of 1 large lemon

2 tablespoons toasted sesame seeds

1 teaspoon ground ginger

1 teaspoon paprika

¾ teaspoon kosher salt

1 (1 ½ pound) London broil (aka top round roast; preferably grass fed)

1 teaspoon extra virgin olive oil

1 Preheat a grill to high.

2 Add the nori and dried chili pepper to a coffee grinder or spice mill. Process them until they are as fine as possible, about 30 seconds. Transfer them to a small bowl and add the lemon zest, sesame seeds, ginger, paprika, and salt. Mix them until they are well combined.

3 Place the steak on a cutting board or large plate. Drizzle ½ teaspoon olive oil on each side, then rub it all over. Sprinkle the seasoning over the steak and rub it in all over to evenly cover the steak. Grill the steak to desired doneness, about 3–5 minutes per side for medium rare. Tent the steak for 5 minutes, then slice it into very thin slices, cutting it on an angle and against the grain. Enjoy immediately.

Cook's Notes

Use a coffee grinder designated just for spices to chop the nori and chili pepper for this recipe if you have one. If you don't have one just for spices and you want to use the coffee grinder you use for your coffee, you can pulse a scrap of bread in the grinder when you're finished chopping your nori and chilies. The bread will remove residual oils from the chilies, making the grinder ready for your morning coffee.

Look for Japones peppers in the international aisle of your grocery store.

Leaner cuts of meat can be really tough if you don't cook, rest, and slice them correctly. Need some chef secrets to help ensure you make this delicious roast in the best way possible? I'm happy to help! Just visit me at **www.devinalexander.com/diabetes** for video demos.

CHOICES/EXCHANGES
3 lean protein

PER SERVING
140 calories, 6 g fat, 1.6 g saturated fat, 0 g trans fat, 50 mg cholesterol, 250 mg sodium, 240 mg potassium, 2 g carbohydrate, 1 g fiber, 0 g sugars, 25 g protein, 150 mg phosphorus

JAPANESE LONDON BROIL

Spice Grilled London Broil

It's always best to tent meats with foil and let them rest after they're cooked, before cutting into them. This resting period allows the juices to redistribute back into the meat, so the juices won't all seep out onto your cutting board. Whatever you do, don't seal the foil around the plate of meat. This steams the meat. Visit me at www.devinalexander.com/diabetes for a quick video demo. I'll also show you what it means to "cut against the grain" of the meat (which is an important technique, especially with lean cuts of meat, used to help keep meat tender).

1 tablespoon paprika

¾ teaspoon kosher salt

1 teaspoon freshly ground
   black pepper

1 teaspoon packed brown sugar

½ teaspoon onion powder

½ teaspoon garlic powder

¼ teaspoon chili powder

⅛ teaspoon ground cayenne

1 teaspoon extra virgin olive oil

1 (1 ½ pound) trimmed London broil
   (aka top round roast; preferably
   grass fed)

1. In a small bowl, combine the paprika, salt, black pepper, brown sugar, onion powder, garlic powder, chili powder, and cayenne.

2. Rub the olive oil over the steak. Then rub the spices into the meat to coat it. Transfer the steak to a resealable plastic bag and refrigerate it for at least 2 hours or overnight.

3. Preheat the grill to high.

4. Remove the seasoned steak from the refrigerator and bring it to room temperature (just for 15 minutes). Remove the steak from the bag and place it on the grill. Grill it until desired doneness is reached, about 3–5 minutes per side for medium rare.

5. Transfer the steak to a plate and cover it loosely with foil. Let it rest for 5 minutes. Slice it against the grain, holding your knife at a 45 degree angle, into thin slices and serve immediately or refrigerate it in an airtight plastic container for up to 3 days. You can also slice it extremely thin and serve on sandwiches.

CHOICES/EXCHANGES
3 lean protein

PER SERVING
150 calories, 4 g fat, 1.3 g saturated fat, 0 g trans fats, 60 mg cholesterol, 270 mg sodium, 260 mg potassium, 2 g carbohydrate, 1 g fiber, 1 g sugars, 24 g protein, 155 mg phosphorus

Honey Lime Marinated London Broil

We all know that Mexican food tends to be on the very heavy side. I try to avoid eating at Mexican restaurants even though they house some of my all time favorite flavors. This recipe is much more subtle in flavor than others in this book and much leaner than many other marinades, but it has a Mexican flair! If you love mild flavors, you will absolutely love this one (my mother does!). The milder flavor profile makes the leftovers a great option for so many other dishes—salads, sandwiches, quesadillas, and tacos—with a fraction of the sodium, fat, and calories normally found in these dishes.

¼ cup freshly squeezed lime juice

2 tablespoons extra virgin olive oil

1 tablespoon plus 1 teaspoon honey

2 tablespoons freshly minced garlic

1 teaspoon kosher salt

1 (1 ¼ pound) trimmed London broil (aka top round roast; preferably grass fed)

1 Whisk the lime juice, olive oil, and honey in a small bowl. Stir in the garlic and salt.

2 Place the steak in a large resealable plastic bag. Pour the marinade over top. Seal the bag and rotate it so the steak is completely covered with the marinade. Place the bag in the refrigerator and marinate the steak for at least 6 hours or overnight, rotating it occasionally, if possible.

3 Preheat a grill to high.

4 Remove the steak from the marinade and place it on the grill. Discard the remaining marinade. Grill it until the desired doneness is reached, about 3–5 minutes per side for medium rare.

5 Place the steak on a plate or cutting board, cover it loosely with foil (tent it), and let it rest for 5 minutes. Slice it into very thin slices, cutting on an angle and against the grain, and enjoy immediately. Or refrigerate the uncut steak in an airtight container for up to 3 days and slice it just before serving.

CHOICES/EXCHANGES

3 lean protein

PER SERVING

150 calories, 4.5 g fat, 1.3 g saturated fat, 0 g trans fat, 60 mg cholesterol, 125 mg sodium, 220 mg potassium, 2 g carbohydrate, 0 g fiber, 1 g sugars, 24 g protein, 150 mg phosphorus

CROCKPOT CHIPOTLE STEAK SIMMER

Crockpot Chipotle Steak Simmer

1 ½ pounds cubed (1 inch cubes) London broil (aka top round roast; preferably grass fed)

½ teaspoon salt free Mexican seasoning

¼ teaspoon kosher salt

2 canned chipotle peppers in adobo sauce

½ tablespoon sauce from canned chipotle peppers in adobo sauce

2 cups canned crushed tomatoes

1 tablespoon Worcestershire sauce

1 tablespoon packed light or dark brown sugar

1 teaspoon plus 1 teaspoon plus 1 teaspoon olive oil, divided

1 ½ cups 1 inch red onion squares

1 ½ cups 1 inch poblano pepper squares

1 teaspoon freshly minced garlic

1 Add the steak cubes to a medium bowl. Season them with the seasoning and salt until evenly coated. Set them aside.

2 Remove 2 chipotle peppers from the can. On a clean cutting board, chop them as finely as possible. Transfer them to a medium bowl. Add ½ tablespoon of the sauce from the can along with the crushed tomatoes, Worcestershire, and brown sugar, and stir to combine. Set the mixture aside.

3 Place a large nonstick frying pan over medium heat. When hot, add 1 teaspoon of the olive oil, the onion, poblano pepper squares, and garlic. Spread them into as even a layer as possible. Cook until they are crisp tender, stirring occasionally so they get evenly cooked. Then transfer them to a crockpot.

4 Return the pan to the heat and add another 1 teaspoon of olive oil. Use a basting brush to distribute the oil evenly over the bottom of the pan. Add half of the seasoned beef cubes. Cook them about 1 minute per side, until browned on all sides. Add the meat to the crockpot.

5 Add the remaining 1 teaspoon of olive oil to the pan, and cook the second half of the seasoned beef cubes for about 1 minute per side. When browned on all sides, add the meat to the crockpot. Then stir in the crushed tomato and adobo mixture. Turn the crockpot on low. Make sure the meat is as submerged as possible in the liquid. Simmer until the meat easily pulls apart with a fork, at least 2–4 hours depending on your crockpot.

6 Enjoy immediately. Try this entrée over amaranth, lean garlic mashed potatoes, or brown rice if your meal plan allows.

recipe continued on next page »

Cook's Notes

Don't know what a poblano pepper is? It's a dark green mild chili pepper. Some grocery stores in the U.S. label them as pasilla peppers, which is actually incorrect. But if your grocery store says they don't carry poblanos and they do carry pasillas, look to see if the "pasillas" are a dark green fresh (not dried) pepper. If so, use the pasillas. Still not sure what to buy? Visit **www.devinalexander.com/diabetes** to see an example. Or green bell peppers can be substituted for the poblanos and will yield a dish that is slightly milder.

Not familiar with the term "crisp tender"? It means that you don't want your veggies hard, but you don't want them to be limp.

If you have a crockpot or multi cooker with browning capability, brown the beef, onions, and peppers in that and skip using the pan altogether.

CHOICES/EXCHANGES
3 nonstarchy vegetable, 3 lean protein

PER SERVING
190 calories, 6 g fat, 2 g saturated fat, 0 g trans fat, 50 mg cholesterol, 390 mg sodium, 570 mg potassium, 13 g carbohydrate, 2 g fiber, 7 g sugars, 26 g protein, 195 mg phosphorus

Mom's Favorite Meatloaf

Olive oil spray (propellant free)

⅓ cup old fashioned oats

¼ cup fat free milk

1 large egg white (preferably cage free)

⅓ cup peeled and shredded carrots, excess water squeezed out

⅓ cup finely chopped whole green onions

1 (4 ounce) jar pimentos, drained very well and chopped finely

¼ cup finely chopped fresh parsley leaves

2 tablespoons finely chopped jalapeño pepper

1 tablespoon Worcestershire sauce

1 teaspoon freshly minced garlic

¼ teaspoon salt

¼ teaspoon reduced sodium salt substitute

1 pound 96% lean ground beef (preferably grass fed)

¼ cup low sodium ketchup

1 Preheat the oven to 350°F.

2 Lightly mist a standard loaf pan (8 ½ × 4 ½ inches) with spray.

3 In a medium mixing bowl, stir the oats, milk, and egg white until well combined. Let them stand for 3 minutes, or until the oats are softened. Stir in the carrots, green onions, pimentos, parsley, jalapeño, Worcestershire, garlic, salt, and reduced sodium salt substitute. Add the beef and mix it until well combined.

4 Transfer the mixture to the prepared loaf pan, flattening the top. Spread the ketchup evenly over the top. Bake until the loaf is just barely pink inside, about 40–50 minutes.

5 Remove the meatloaf from the oven and let it stand for 5 minutes. Slice the loaf into 8 equal slices. Enjoy immediately.

Cook's Notes

Never used a salt substitute before? There are a lot of different products on the market. Some are great, others are not so great. Want to know which brand I currently love? Visit me at www.devinalexander.com/diabetes and I'll reveal that along with chef secrets and so much more!

CHOICES/EXCHANGES
1 carbohydrate, 4 lean protein

PER SERVING
230 calories, 6 g fat, 2.5 g saturated fat, 0.3 g trans fat, 105 mg cholesterol, 430 mg sodium, 780 mg potassium, 14 g carbohydrate, 2 g fiber, 7 g sugars, 28 g protein, 315 mg phosphorus

Rosemary Beef Stew

1 tablespoon whole grain oat flour

⅛ teaspoon sea salt

Freshly ground black pepper, to taste

1 pound trimmed London broil (aka top round roast; preferably grass fed), cut into ¾ inch cubes

1 teaspoon plus ½ teaspoon extra virgin olive oil, divided

1 small onion, cut into chunks (about 1 ¾ cups)

5 medium cloves garlic, peeled and sliced as thinly as possible

2 cups lower sodium beef broth

1 cup low sodium beef broth (plus up to an additional ½ cup if needed)

1 sprig rosemary

2 medium carrots (about ¾ pound), peeled and cut into ½ inch rounds (about 2 ¼ cups)

1 pound peeled light fleshed sweet potatoes, cut into 1 inch chunks (about 3 ½ cups)

½ pound 1 inch asparagus pieces (about 2 cups)

1 In a medium bowl, sprinkle the flour, salt, and pepper over the beef cubes. Toss until the beef is evenly coated.

2 Preheat a large nonstick soup pot over medium high heat. Add 1 teaspoon of the oil, then the beef cubes. Brown the beef cubes on all sides, approximately 1 minute per side.

3 Turn heat to medium and add the remaining ½ teaspoon of oil, the onions, and the garlic. Cook them until the onions are tender, approximately 5 minutes, stirring occasionally with a wooden spoon and scraping any brown bits from the bottom of the pan as you do.

4 Add both broths, the rosemary, and the carrots to the pot. When the broth comes to a boil, turn the heat to medium low and cover the pot (the broth should still be boiling slightly). Cook for 45 minutes. Add the potatoes, then continue cooking until the potatoes are tender and the meat comes apart with a fork, about an additional 30–45 minutes.

5 Meanwhile, a few minutes before the stew is finished, fill a small soup pot half full with water and place it over medium high heat. When the water comes to a boil, add the asparagus and boil it until crisp tender (about 1–3 minutes depending on the size of the pieces).

6 Season the stew with additional pepper, if desired. Remove and discard the rosemary sprig. Portion out about 1 ½ cups of stew per bowl, adding about ½ cup asparagus to each if you plan to enjoy it immediately. Otherwise, store the stew and the asparagus separately and add the asparagus just prior to enjoying it.

Cook's Notes

If you taste the meat for this stew right after you sear it, it will be tough. Sometime during cooking, usually between 1 ½–2 hours of cooking it at a very low boil in broth, it will become extremely tender—the meat breaks down and becomes so tender it will literally fall apart when pulled with forks. If it's tough when you go to serve it, it wasn't cooked long enough.

Depending what pan you use and how high the heat is (it should just be simmering during cooking, not on a full boil), you may need additional broth to ensure that all the ingredients are submerged when you add the potatoes.

You could add the asparagus in the stew during the last few minutes of cooking, but the asparagus can overpower the other flavors in the stew, especially if you're enjoying any of the stew as leftovers. So if you're not a huge fan of asparagus (or your partner or children aren't), I strongly recommend taking the extra step to cook the asparagus separately. Alternatively, if you happen to have leftover steamed or grilled asparagus, you can add that instead.

CHOICES/EXCHANGES
1 ½ starch, 2 nonstarchy vegetable,
3 lean protein

PER SERVING
290 calories, 6 g fat, 2 g saturated fat, 0 g trans fat, 50 mg cholesterol, 470 mg sodium, 620 mg potassium, 34 g carbohydrate, 6 g fiber, 9 g sugars, 31 g protein, 200 mg phosphorous

Java London Broil

I love this recipe and I really wanted to include it in this book! But it does come with a tiny caveat: you may need to experiment with the kind of coffee you use. If you use a super bold coffee bean that is very fresh, it could be a bit bitter. But if you use coffee that has been sitting around forever and it's a really mild blend to begin with, it might not be quite as flavorful as you'd like. So, bear that in mind and feel free to adjust the type and amount of coffee as needed. I've made this London broil multiple times with multiple blends of coffee and 2 teaspoons of coffee seems to be the right balance to me.

2 teaspoons freshly ground coffee

½ tablespoon stevia brown sugar blend (such as Truvia Brown Sugar Blend)

2 teaspoons freshly ground black pepper

1 teaspoon ground coriander

½ teaspoon dried oregano

¼ teaspoon sea salt

1 (1 ½ pound) London broil (aka top round roast; preferably grass fed)

1 teaspoon extra virgin olive oil

1 Preheat a grill to high.

2 To a small bowl, add the coffee, brown sugar blend, black pepper, coriander, oregano, and salt. Mix well.

3 Place the steak on a cutting board or large plate. Drizzle ½ teaspoon of olive oil on each side of the steak, then rub it all over. Sprinkle the seasoning mixture over the steak and rub it in to evenly cover the steak.

4 Grill the steak to desired doneness, about 3–5 minutes per side for medium rare. Tent the steak with foil for 5 minutes then slice it into very thin slices, cutting on an angle and against the grain. Enjoy immediately.

Cook's Notes

It's always best to tent meats with foil after they're cooked, before cutting into them. This resting period allows the juice to redistribute back into the meat, instead of letting it all seep out onto your cutting board. However, make sure you don't "seal" the foil around the plate of meat; this steams the meat.

CHOICES/EXCHANGES
3 lean protein

PER SERVING
150 calories, 4 g fat, 1.2 g saturated fat, 0 g trans fat, 60 mg cholesterol, 120 mg sodium, 230 mg potassium, 2 g carbohydrate, 0 g fiber, 1 g sugars, 24 g protein, 150 mg phosphorous

Herb Butter Rubbed Turkey Breast

You might wonder why I call for bone in turkey breast in this recipe given that the bone creates extra work. It's true, it does. But it is worth the extra effort, as it tends to be easier to yield a perfectly cooked turkey breast when it's still on the bone. That being said, it's also important that you know how to use a meat thermometer when cooking this turkey breast. If you do it wrong, it will read wrong, and you could end up with an undercooked or overcooked bird. Don't know how to use a meat thermometer or worried because you don't even own one? Worry no more. Just visit me at www.devinalexander.com/diabetes for a quick tutorial! The last thing I want is for you to eat dry turkey!

Olive oil spray (propellant free)

1 (2 ¼ pound) bone in turkey breast half (preferably free range)

1 ½ tablespoons vegan butter (from a stick, not a tub), room temperature

2 teaspoons very finely chopped fresh thyme leaves

2 teaspoons very finely chopped fresh tarragon leaves

2 teaspoons very finely chopped fresh rosemary leaves

1 teaspoon very finely chopped fresh sage leaves

¼ teaspoon sea salt

⅛ teaspoon freshly ground black pepper

1 Preheat the oven to 350°F. Mist a 9 × 9 inch casserole or baking dish with spray.

2 Place the turkey on a cutting board and remove all of the skin and any visible fat. Using a fork, poke the breast 25 times evenly over each side as deep as the tines of the fork.

3 In a small bowl, mix the butter, thyme, tarragon, rosemary, sage, salt, and pepper with a fork until well combined. Place the breast, bone side up, on the cutting board and use your fingers to rub about ¼ of the herbed butter evenly over the visible meat (don't rub over the bone). Flip the breast over and place it in the prepared baking dish. Rub the remaining herbed butter evenly over the top and sides of the breast. Without touching the breast, carefully pour ¼ cup of water into the bottom of the pan (this will help keep the turkey moist).

4 Cook the breast for about 40–50 minutes or until a thermometer inserted into the breast reads 175°F and it is no longer pink inside.

5 Remove the turkey from the oven and loosely tent it with foil for about 10 minutes to allow the juices to redistribute (the breast will continue cooking to reach 180°F while standing). Transfer it to a cutting board. Slice the turkey into thin slices, cutting on an angle and against the grain. Enjoy immediately (if you plan on using leftovers as deli meat, only slice the portion you are about to eat, then refrigerate the remainder of the breast and slice it as thinly as possible before eating).

CHOICES/EXCHANGES
4 lean protein

PER SERVING
190 calories, 5 g fat, 1.4 g saturated fat, 0 g trans fat, 85 mg cholesterol, 220 mg sodium, 280 mg potassium, 0 g carbohydrate, 0 g fiber, 0 g sugars, 33 g protein, 250 mg phosphorous

Sriracha Mayo Roasted Turkey Breast

Sriracha has obviously become super trendy in recent years. Your gut reaction to seeing it in this recipe might be "Oh, that's going to be too spicy!" But just give it a try on this one. There are only 2 teaspoons of sriracha on this turkey breast, which is over 2 pounds, and it's mixed with mayo. I promise this turkey isn't spicy. It does have a tiny hint of kick, but that's all, and only in the bites that actually have the mayo rubbed on them. The mayo helps keep the breast nice and tender and the sriracha provides a mild (I promise) delicious flavor in this instance!

Olive oil spray (propellant free)

1 (2 ¼ pound) bone in turkey breast half (preferably free range)

2 tablespoons light mayonnaise (preferably natural)

2 teaspoons sriracha sauce (preferably natural)

Cook's Notes

It's important to use a spray without propellants so you can spray directly onto your food. I often spray olive oil directly onto food (as you'll see in many of these recipes). Most of the prefilled olive oil sprays in cans at the grocery store that you may have been using forever contain propellants and other ingredients so they warn that you cannot spray them directly onto your food. Even if you don't spray these products directly onto your food, the propellants are still touching your food when you cook with the spray. So what are you supposed to buy? Visit me at **www.devinalexander.com/diabetes** where I provide suggestions and so much more.

1 Preheat the oven to 350°F. Mist a 9 × 9 inch casserole or baking dish with spray.

2 Place the turkey on a cutting board and remove all of the skin and any visible fat. Using a fork, poke the breast 25 times evenly over each side as deep as the tines of the fork.

3 In a small bowl, stir the mayonnaise and sriracha until well combined. Place the breast, bone side up, on the cutting board and, using a pastry brush (or your fingers if you don't have one), rub about ⅓ of the mayonnaise mixture evenly over the meat (don't rub it over the bone). Flip the breast over and place it in the prepared baking dish. Brush the remaining mayonnaise mixture evenly over the top and sides of the breast. Without touching the breast, carefully pour ¼ cup of water into the bottom of the pan (this will help keep it moist).

4 Cook the breast until a thermometer inserted into it reads 175°F and it is no longer pink inside, about 35–50 minutes.

5 Remove the turkey from the oven and loosely tent it with foil for about 10 minutes to allow the juices to redistribute (the breast will continue cooking to reach 180°F while standing). Transfer it to a cutting board. Slice the turkey into thin slices, cutting on a diagonal and against the grain (if you plan on using leftovers as deli meat, only slice the portion you are about to eat, then refrigerate the remainder of the breast and slice it as thinly as possible before eating).

CHOICES/EXCHANGES
4 lean protein

PER SERVING
170 calories, 3.5 g fat, 0.8 g saturated fat, 0 g trans fat, 90 mg cholesterol, 180 mg sodium, 270 mg potassium, 1 g carbohydrate, 0 g fiber, 1 g sugars, 33 g protein, 250 mg phosphorous

SRIRACHA MAYO ROASTED TURKEY BREAST

Mediterranean Meatballs with Creamy Dill Sauce

Be sure not to overcook the meatballs in this recipe! You want them cooked so they are no longer pink inside, but if you cook them past that, you'll dry them out. If you are not able to touch them and tell whether or not they're done, just cut into one after 10 minutes of cooking time, and then continue cooking and checking them 1 minute at a time until they're done. If they begin to dry out in your oven, you can always put a cake pan ⅔ filled with water in the oven. This will help keep them moist.

⅓ cup old fashioned oats

3 large egg whites (preferably cage free)

1 pound 99% lean ground turkey (preferably free range)

2 tablespoons lemon zest (fine zest, not thick ribbons)

1 teaspoon freshly minced garlic

2 teaspoons very finely chopped rosemary leaves

1 teaspoon very finely chopped sage leaves

¾ teaspoon freshly ground black pepper

½ teaspoon kosher salt

Olive oil spray (propellant free)

¾ cup Garlicky Dill Dip & Sauce (see page 181)

*If you have the Garlicky Dill Dip & Sauce prepared.

1 Preheat the oven to 350°F. Line a large baking sheet with nonstick foil.

2 In a medium mixing bowl, combine the oats and the egg whites. Add the turkey, lemon zest, garlic, rosemary, sage, black pepper, and salt. With a fork or your hands, mix the ingredients together until well combined. Portion the mixture into 20 balls (about 1 ounce each; use a 1 ½ inch meatball scoop for ease if you have one). Roll the balls by hand, slightly dampening your hands, if necessary, to prevent the mixture from sticking to them.

3 Place the meatballs, not touching, on the prepared baking sheet. Lightly mist them with the spray. Bake them for 6 minutes, flip them, then continue baking them until they are no longer pink inside, about 5–8 minutes.

4 Place 3 tablespoons of the sauce on each of 4 plates, spreading it over an area large enough to place the meatballs on the sauce. Place 5 meatballs on each "bed" of sauce. Enjoy immediately.

CHOICES/EXCHANGES
½ carbohydrate, 4 lean protein

PER SERVING
220 calories, 6 g fat, 1.2 g saturated fat, 0 g trans fat, 65 mg cholesterol, 470 mg sodium, 460 mg potassium, 7 g carbohydrate, 1 g fiber, 1 g sugars, 36 g protein, 340 mg phosphorous

Satay Grilled Chicken Breast

I try to make almost every meal I cook at home look as appealing as every dish I served in my restaurant. You'll notice that elegant restaurants almost never completely cover a chicken breast or steak with sauce. Instead they generally pour it over the center one third of the protein—so you can see the protein—and then let the rest drip down the sides.

1 (4 ounce) trimmed, boneless, skinless chicken breast (preferably free range)

Olive oil spray (propellant free)

½ teaspoon salt free Szechuan seasoning

1/16 teaspoon sea salt

½ cup (about 1 ounce) spiralized, unpeeled cucumber

½ cup (about ¾ ounce) spiralized carrot

3 tablespoons warmed Peanut Satay Sauce (see page 189)

*If you have the Peanut Satay Sauce prepared.

1 Preheat a grill to high.

2 Place the chicken breast between 2 sheets of plastic wrap or wax paper on a flat work surface. Using the flat side of a meat mallet, pound the chicken breast to ½ inch thickness. Spray both sides with spray. Season both sides evenly with the seasoning and salt.

3 Grill the chicken until it's no longer pink inside, about 3–5 minutes per side.

4 Mix the cucumber and carrot curls together and spread them on a dinner plate so they act as a bed for the chicken breast. Place the grilled chicken breast on top. Drizzle the satay sauce over the center one third of the chicken breast. Enjoy immediately.

Cook's Notes

Depending on the spiralizer you use, it may yield "noodles" that are long enough to jump rope with! Ha! But seriously, you may want to cut the cucumber and carrot spirals into spaghetti length pieces if they're really long.

CHOICES/EXCHANGES
½ carbohydrate, 4 lean protein, 1 fat

PER SERVING
260 calories, 12 g fat, 2.5 g saturated fat, 0 g trans fat, 65 mg cholesterol, 420 mg sodium, 480 mg potassium, 9 g carbohydrate, 2 g fiber, 4 g sugars, 29 g protein, 270 mg phosphorus

UPDATED POTATO CHIP CRUSTED CHICKEN

Updated Potato Chip Crusted Chicken

I first ran a version of this recipe in my book The Most Decadent Diet Ever! *and it was a huge hit! I've since updated it. The key elements to making this dish are making sure you soak the chicken in buttermilk for at least 6 hours to allow it to become nice and tender. The second is not to overcook the chicken. When it's no longer pink inside, it's done. Beyond that point, you're just drying it out. And, in this case, the extra moisture that gets expelled if it's overcooked will make the breading fall off and/or become soggy!*

2 (4 ounce) boneless, skinless chicken breasts (preferably free range), visible fat removed

⅓ cup low fat buttermilk

½ teaspoon onion powder

¼ teaspoon paprika

⅛ teaspoon freshly ground black pepper

⅛ teaspoon kosher salt

1/32 teaspoon cayenne, or more to taste

1/32 teaspoon garlic powder

1 ½ ounces (about ½ cup) finely crushed baked potato chips (preferably natural)

Olive oil spray (propellant free)

1 Place the chicken breasts between 2 sheets of plastic wrap or wax paper on a flat work surface. Using the flat side of a meat mallet, pound them to an even ½ inch thickness.

2 Transfer the chicken breasts to a resealable plastic bag that is slightly larger than the breasts. Pour the buttermilk over the breasts, seal the bag, and then turn the bag to coat the chicken. Refrigerate for at least 6 hours or overnight, rotating once or twice if possible. Note: It is super important to soak the chicken; it's what will make it tender!

3 Preheat the oven to 450°F. Line a small baking sheet with nonstick foil.

4 Mix the onion powder, paprika, black pepper, salt, cayenne, and garlic powder in a small bowl. Add the chips to a medium shallow bowl.

5 Remove one chicken breast from the buttermilk and let any excess buttermilk drip off. Sprinkle both sides of the breast evenly with half of the seasoning mixture. Then transfer the breast to the bowl of crushed chips and cover it on all sides with the chips. Place the coated breast on the prepared baking sheet. Repeat with the remaining chicken breast and seasoning. Discard any remaining buttermilk. Press any remaining chips into the tops of the breasts.

recipe continued on next page »

6 Lightly mist the top of both breasts with spray. Bake them for 6 minutes, then carefully flip the breasts with a spatula, being sure not to remove the coating. Lightly mist the tops with spray and bake for 4–7 minutes until the coating is crispy and the chicken is no longer pink inside. Enjoy immediately.

Cook's Notes

It's really easy to crush the chips if you put them in a resealable plastic bag and pound them with the flat side of a meat mallet or a rolling pin. They need to be pretty finely crushed (like coarse bread crumbs) or you won't be able to coat the breasts completely.

CHOICES/EXCHANGES
1 starch, 3 lean protein

PER SERVING
220 calories, 4.5 g fat, 1.4 g saturated fat, 0 g trans fat, 65 mg cholesterol, 290 mg sodium, 420 mg potassium, 18 g carbohydrate, 2 g fiber, 2 g sugars, 26 g protein, 245 mg phosphorous

Grilled Harissa Chicken Skewers

1 pound chicken breasts (preferably free range), trimmed of all visible fat and pounded to ¼ inch thickness

2 tablespoons fat free Greek yogurt

1 ½–2 tablespoons jarred harissa

¼ teaspoon kosher salt

16 wooden or metal skewers

Olive oil spray (propellant free)

½ cup Renovated Ranch (see page 184)

*If you have the Renovated Ranch prepared.

1 If using wooden skewers, soak the skewers in water for at least 1 hour or overnight.

2 Preheat a grill to high.

3 Cut the chicken into 16 equal strips. In a small mixing bowl, toss the strips in the yogurt, harissa, and salt until all ingredients are well combined. Allow them to marinate for 30 minutes in the refrigerator. Thread the chicken onto the skewers. Lightly mist both sides of skewers with spray.

4 Turn the grill to low, if possible. Place the chicken on the grill (away from direct flame if the grill can't be turned to low). Grill the strips until no longer pink throughout, about 2–3 minutes per side. Transfer the skewers to a serving platter and add the dip to a serving bowl or divide the skewers and dip among 4 individual plates. Enjoy immediately.

Cook's Notes

Harissa is a chili pepper paste that has become increasingly popular in the U.S. in recent years. It's great for creating a quick entrée or adding a bit of spice to many dishes. Unlike Asian chili pastes that can have as many as 700–1,000 mg of sodium per tablespoon, I've found harissa to have only about 150 mg of sodium per tablespoon.

If you are eating these chicken skewers without sauce and aren't a huge spicy food fan, add only 1 ½ tablespoons of the harissa to the recipe. But if you like food with a bit of a kick and plan to dip the chicken in ranch, as suggested, you'll love it with 2 tablespoons of harissa.

CHOICES/EXCHANGES
4 lean protein

PER SERVING
180 calories, 4 g fat, 1 g saturated fat, 0 g trans fat, 70 mg cholesterol, 390 mg sodium, 325 mg potassium, 4 g carbohydrate, 0 g fiber, 1 g sugars, 28 g protein, 225 mg phosphorus

GIFT WRAPPED MANDARIN CHICKEN

Gift Wrapped Mandarin Chicken

If you've ever had gift wrapped chicken in a Chinese restaurant, you likely know that it's usually an appetizer and the chicken triangles are tiny, containing just a morsel of delicious chicken—and, unfortunately, a ton of sodium. In this recipe I give these "packages" a twist, making them large enough to enclose an entire chicken breast and using a mandarin orange marinade. Don't know how to gift wrap the chicken? Or don't know how (or why) to pound the chicken? Visit me at www.devinalexander.com/diabetes where I show you!

3 tablespoons frozen orange juice concentrate, thawed

2 tablespoons lower sodium soy sauce

½ cup canned unsweetened mandarin oranges with juice

2 teaspoons stevia honey blend sweetener (such as Truvia Nectar)

2 teaspoons chili garlic sauce (preferably natural; found in international section of most major grocery stores)

2 teaspoons toasted or roasted sesame oil

3 medium cloves garlic, peeled and minced

4 (4 ounce) trimmed, boneless, skinless chicken breasts (preferably free range), pounded to ½ inch thickness

1 In a medium resealable plastic or glass container, whisk together the juice concentrate, soy sauce, the liquid from the mandarin oranges (refrigerate the actual oranges in a different resealable container until they are ready to be added to the foil pouches), sweetener, chili garlic sauce, and sesame oil. Stir in the garlic. Add the chicken, submerging it in the marinade. Cover the container and marinate the chicken in the refrigerator for at least 6 hours or overnight.

2 Preheat the oven to 400°F.

3 Tear a 12 × 12 inch sturdy piece of aluminum foil and place it on a clean work surface in front of you so that one of the points is facing you. Lay a piece of chicken in the center of the foil (your goal is going to be to create a triangular, standing "pouch" that holds the chicken, oranges, and marinade).

4 Temporarily fold the sides up just enough to keep the liquid from spilling out. Add ¼ of the mandarin oranges to the pouch. Spoon ¼ of remaining marinade over the chicken breast.

recipe continued on next page »

5 Now, grab the points closest to you and opposite to you and lift them up over the breast so they meet, still being careful that the liquid does not spill out. Fold the edges so they close, forming a triangle, and make sure they are not touching the breast (except where the breast sits on the foil). Repeat this procedure to wrap the 3 remaining breasts and the remaining oranges and marinade.

6 Place the pouches side by side, not touching, on a baking sheet or baking pan. Bake them until the chicken is no longer pink inside, about 12–16 minutes. Be super careful not to burn yourself with the steam from the pouches as you open them. Enjoy immediately.

CHOICES/EXCHANGES
1 carbohydrate, 3 lean protein

PER SERVING
200 calories, 4 g fat, 7 g saturated fat, 0 g trans fat, 65 mg cholesterol, 310 mg sodium, 450 mg potassium, 12 g carbohydrate, 0 g fiber, 10 g sugars, 27 g protein, 245 mg phosphorus

Grilled Chicken Zoodle Marinara

If you "cook" the zucchini in this recipe, it starts to taste like zucchini. If you just warm it and toss it in the hot marinara, it won't taste like zucchini, so it's a great, nutritious dish for non-veggie lovers. I love love love Pecorino Romano cheese, but it's generally high in sodium. So if you have high blood pressure or need to watch your sodium intake, I'd definitely opt for Parmesan in this recipe.

1 medium zucchini (about 8 ounces), ends trimmed or 6 ½ ounces store bought zucchini spirals

1 (4 ounce) trimmed, boneless, skinless chicken breast (preferably free range), pounded to ½ inch thickness

½ teaspoon extra virgin olive oil

½ teaspoon salt free garlic and herb bread seasoning

1/16 teaspoon sea salt

Freshly ground black pepper, to taste

Olive oil spray (propellant free)

¾ cup all natural marinara sauce (preferably low fat, low salt, no sugar added); heated

1 tablespoon (about ¼ ounce) grated Parmesan or Pecorino Romano cheese (preferably natural)

1 Preheat a grill to medium.

2 Cut the zucchini into pieces according to the directions for your spiralizer (if you purchased zucchini spirals then skip this step). Create "spaghetti" noodles from the pieces using a spiralizer. Let the spiralized zucchini rest on a lint free towel or paper towels.

3 Rub the chicken evenly all over with the olive oil, then the seasoning, salt, and pepper. Place the chicken on the grill and turn the heat to low (if there is no temperature control, place it away from direct flame). Grill it until it is no longer pink inside, about 3–5 minutes per side.

4 Remove the chicken from the grill and tent it, letting it rest for 3 minutes. Transfer it to a cutting board and cut it diagonally across the breast to create ½ inch strips.

5 Meanwhile, place a small nonstick frying pan over medium heat. When it's hot, remove it from the burner just long enough to lightly mist it with spray. Toss the zucchini in the pan just long enough to warm it—do not cook it or it will get mushy.

6 Transfer the warmed zucchini to a strainer for a minute to release any excess moisture. Then transfer it to a serving plate. Top it with the marinara sauce. Place the chicken breast on top. Season it with the cheese and additional pepper, if desired, and enjoy immediately.

CHOICES/EXCHANGES
1 ½ starch, 4 lean protein, ½ fat

PER SERVING
300 calories, 10 g fat, 2 g saturated fat, 0 g trans fat, 70 mg cholesterol, 250 mg sodium, 1250 mg potassium, 20 g carbohydrate, 10 g fiber, 11 g sugars, 30 g protein, 335 mg phosphorus

Margarita Chicken

People are often surprised when they learn that I drink alcohol, in moderation, of course, given my "healthy" outlook on life. But being healthy doesn't mean living a life of deprivation. That's why I refer to my work as "Devinly"; it's healthy and heavenly…and made by Devin! A healthy lifestyle should be fun and food should bring joy! I'm a big margarita fan, so I thought I'd infuse a bit of my love for those flavors into this delicious chicken dish! It's a great one for parties!

3 tablespoons freshly squeezed orange juice

2 tablespoons freshly squeezed lime juice

2 tablespoons olive oil

1 tablespoon tequila

1 teaspoon freshly minced garlic

1 ½ teaspoons seeded, freshly minced jalapeño

½ teaspoon chili powder

½ teaspoon kosher salt

6 (4 ounce) trimmed, boneless, skinless chicken breasts (preferably free range)

Lime slices, for garnish

1 In a small mixing bowl, whisk together the orange juice, lime juice, olive oil, tequila, garlic, jalapeño, chili powder, and salt until well combined.

2 Add the chicken to a large resealable plastic bag. Pour the marinade over the chicken. Seal the bag and press any air from it. Then massage the marinade around the chicken breasts to make sure they're completely coated. Refrigerate the bag for at least 6 hours or overnight.

3 Preheat a grill to high heat.

4 When hot, place the chicken breasts side by side on the grill (if using a charcoal grill, place the breasts away from direct flame; if using a gas grill, turn the heat to medium after the chicken has been placed on the grill). Discard any remaining marinade. Grill the breasts until no longer pink inside, about 3–5 minutes per side. Garnish with lime slices. Enjoy immediately.

CHOICES/EXCHANGES
3 lean protein

PER SERVING
150 calories, 3 g fat, 1 g saturated fat, 0 g trans fat, 65 mg cholesterol, 170 mg sodium, 305 mg potassium, 1 g carbohydrate, 0 g fiber, 1 g sugars, 26 g protein, 225 mg phosphorus

MARGARITA CHICKEN

Chicken Pinwheels with Sundried Tomatoes & Goat Cheese

1 ounce dried sundried tomatoes (not oil packed)

1 small clove garlic, peeled and minced

4 (4 ounce) boneless, skinless chicken breasts (preferably free range), visible fat removed

¼ teaspoon plus ⅛ teaspoon sea salt, divided

1 ½ ounces (about 5 tablespoons) crumbled light goat cheese (preferably natural)

¼ cup finely slivered fresh basil leaves (aka basil chiffonade)

Olive oil spray (propellant free)

Freshly ground black pepper, to taste

1 Preheat the oven to 325°F. Line a baking sheet with nonstick foil.

2 Bring a small pot of water to a boil. Add the sundried tomatoes and boil them for approximately 1 minute, or until rehydrated and tender. Drain the tomatoes, then pat them dry with a lint free towel or paper towels.

3 Add the tomatoes along with the garlic to the bowl of a mini food processor fitted with a chopping blade. Process them until the ingredients are very finely chopped (you can do this by hand if you don't have a mini food processor).

4 Lay the chicken breasts, smooth sides up, on a cutting board or flat work surface. Cover them with waxed paper or plastic wrap. Using the flat end of a meat mallet and starting in the center of the breasts, working outward, pound them to ¼ inch thickness.

5 Flip the breasts so the smooth sides (tops of the breasts) are facedown and arrange them so that the pointy ends (tip of the breasts) are closest to you. Sprinkle ¼ teaspoon of the salt evenly over all 4 chicken breasts. Spread ¼ of the tomato mixture (about 1 heaping tablespoon) evenly over each chicken breast, leaving about ½ inch at the thicker end (the end furthest from you) bare. Then sprinkle ¼ (about 1 heaping tablespoon) of the cheese and ¼ of the basil (about 1 tablespoon) evenly over the tomato mixture on each breast.

6 Starting at the end of the chicken breast that is closest to you, carefully roll each chicken breast into a tight roll, being sure to keep the filling inside. Lightly mist the outsides of the breasts with spray, rotating them to mist them all over. Season them evenly all over with the remaining ⅛ teaspoon salt and the pepper.

7 Place a medium nonstick frying pan over medium high heat. When it's hot, remove the pan just long enough to mist it with spray. Carefully place the chicken breasts with the seam sides down in the pan. Cook them until they are a light golden brown and then, using tongs, gently rotate them to lightly brown the entire outsides, about 1 minute per face.

8 Transfer the breasts to the prepared baking sheet and bake them until they are no longer pink inside or until a meat thermometer inserted into chicken reaches 175°F, about 12–18 minutes (varies depending on how much you browned them). Remove them from the oven and tent them with foil for 3 minutes. Cut each into thirds to create 3 pinwheels. Enjoy immediately.

Cook's Notes

Don't know how or even why to pound chicken breasts? Feel like these pinwheels are intimidating? Don't worry! I have you covered! Visit me at **www.devinalexander.com/diabetes** and I'll show you everything you need to know to make the perfect chicken.

When buying sundried tomatoes, be sure to check the labels. Obviously, you don't want to opt for those in oil, but beyond that you might find some surprises. I found one package that had 25 mg of sodium per 1 (½ ounce) serving and another with a whopping 150 mg of sodium for the same sized serving. If I hadn't read the nutritional information, I wouldn't have realized the difference.

It's best to keep goat cheese refrigerated until you are ready to add it to the recipe to ensure that the crumbles get evenly distributed. When sitting at room temperature, goat cheese tends to get super soft and doesn't want to crumble. If you can, I'd recommend buying it already crumbled. Or try putting the amount you plan to use in the freezer for about 15 minutes to make it easier to crumble and distribute evenly. If it doesn't crumble, it's best to spread it (like you'd spread butter).

You can secure the roll with cooking twine or toothpicks if you like. I prefer to just handle them with silicone tipped tongs, which help keep them intact.

CHOICES/EXCHANGES
1 nonstarchy vegetable, 3 lean protein

PER SERVING
180 calories, 6 g fat, 2.4 g saturated fat, 0 g trans fat, 75 mg cholesterol, 420 mg sodium, 450 mg potassium, 5 g carbohydrate, 1 g fiber, 3 g sugars, 27 g protein, 230 mg phosphorus

RANCH SLATHERED CHICKEN & BROCCOLI STUFFED POTATO

Ranch Slathered Chicken & Broccoli Stuffed Potato

I love this dish! It's so simple it's nuts! People who try it always say, "There's no way that's healthy!" In fact, the day we shot the photo, I texted it to a guy who was a producer on Celebrity Apprentice *who I dated a couple of times. He texted back, "If you can make THAT healthy, marry me!" Though I never thought marriage was in the cards with him, it certainly was fun to be able to make it Devinly decadent!*

1 (6 ounce) light fleshed sweet potato, scrubbed clean

1 (4 ounce) chicken breast (preferably free range), trimmed and cut into ½ inch wide strips across the breast

½ teaspoon salt free garlic and herb bread seasoning

¹⁄₁₆ teaspoon reduced sodium salt substitute

Freshly ground black pepper, to taste

8 ounces broccoli florets

Olive oil spray (propellant free)

¼ cup Renovated Ranch (see page 184)

½ tablespoon sliced chives (¼ inch pieces)

Steamer insert/rack

*If you have the Renovated Ranch prepared.

Cook's Notes

You can use a leftover baked sweet potato in this recipe if you have one on hand. Sweet potatoes that are baked in foil reheat very well. So save time by cooking several on Sunday to reheat during the week.

1 Preheat the oven to 425°F.

2 Wrap the potato in foil. Poke it with a fork 4 times and place it on a middle oven rack. Place a sheet of foil or a baking sheet on the rack below the potato (to catch any drippings). Bake it until it is tender throughout, about 45 minutes to 1 hour.

3 When the potato is almost cooked through, mix the chicken, seasoning, salt substitute, and pepper together in a small bowl.

4 Place a steamer insert in a large soup pot. Fill the pot with water so it reaches just below the steamer insert. Place the pot over high heat and bring the water to a boil. Add the broccoli and cover the pot. Cook it until crisp tender, about 2–5 minutes.

5 Place a small nonstick frying pan over medium high heat. When hot, remove the pan from the heat just long enough to mist it with spray. Add the chicken and cook it until it is browned on the outsides and no longer pink inside, about 1–2 minutes per side. If it's getting too browned before it's cooked through, reduce the heat to low to complete cooking.

6 Place the potato in a shallow bowl or on a plate. Cut a slit in the top of the potato that's almost the length of the potato (don't cut it in half) and about ¾ of the way into the potato. Add the chicken to the center of the potato. Place the broccoli around the potato. Slather the dressing over the potato and broccoli. Top the potato with chives. Enjoy immediately.

CHOICES/EXCHANGES

2 starch, 3 nonstarchy vegetable,
4 lean protein

PER SERVING

390 calories, 6 g fat, 1 g saturated fat, 0 g trans fat, 70 mg cholesterol, 460 mg sodium, 1800 mg potassium, 47 g carbohydrate, 12 g fiber, 12 g sugars, 39 g protein, 380 mg phosphorus

Chili, Garlic & Basil Chicken Stir-Fry

This dish is technically not a stir-fry. But I was commissioned to write an article for Men's Fitness *magazine years ago that was loosely based on a traditional stir-fry; it was a huge hit! So I decided to do a twist on that recipe here and I'm just keeping the stir-fry name.*

2 ounces uncooked brown rice udon noodles

1 teaspoon plus ½ teaspoon toasted or roasted sesame oil, divided

2 teaspoons plus ½ teaspoon chili garlic sauce, divided

½ tablespoon freshly squeezed lemon juice

4 ounces chicken breast (preferably free range), cut into bite sized strips

Olive oil spray (propellant free)

1 cup (1 inch) asparagus pieces

½ cup red onion strips

1 teaspoon freshly minced garlic

2–4 medium, fresh basil leaves, or to taste, stems removed and slivered (aka basil chiffonade)

Cook's Notes

Asian cuisine can be a salt bomb. And even with a healthy recipe like this, if you forget to check the label, you may find yourself swollen from a crazy huge sodium intake. I almost accidentally bought udon noodles with 500 mg of sodium per serving and chili garlic sauce with 780 mg of sodium per tablespoon.

CHOICES/EXCHANGES
2 ½ starch, 2 nonstarchy vegetable, 2 lean protein, 1 fat

1 Bring a large pot of water to a boil. Add the udon noodles and cook until they are tender but have a slight "bite" to them, about 6–8 minutes. Drain and toss them in 1 teaspoon of sesame oil.

2 In a small bowl, mix the remaining ½ teaspoon of the sesame oil, 2 teaspoons of the chili garlic sauce, and the lemon juice. Set the mixture aside.

3 Toss the chicken strips in the remaining ½ teaspoon chili garlic sauce.

4 Heat a large nonstick stir-fry pan or wok over medium high heat until hot. Remove the pan from the heat long enough to lightly mist it with spray. Add the asparagus, onion, and garlic. Cook them until the onions are crisp tender and the asparagus is bright green and warmed.

5 Push the veggies to edges of the pan. Respray the center of the pan (again, removing it from the heat to spray) and add the chicken in a single layer. Cook the chicken until it is no longer pink inside, about 1–2 minutes per side. Push the veggies back into center of the pan, mixing them with the chicken. Add the sauce and toss the chicken and veggies in it. Remove from the heat.

6 Spread the cooked noodles evenly in the bottom of a salad bowl or a dinner plate. Spoon the chicken and veggie mixture over the noodles. Top with the basil. Enjoy immediately.

PER SERVING
390 calories, 10 g fat, 1.7 g saturated fat, 0 g trans fat, 65 mg cholesterol, 300 mg sodium, 600 mg potassium, 53 g carbohydrate, 6 g fiber, 6 g sugars, 24 g protein, 380 mg phosphorus

Chicken Cheesesteak Lettuce Cups

*It's very important that you use a sharp knife to shave the chicken for this delicious recipe. Not sure how to shave the chicken properly? Visit **www.devinalexander.com/diabetes** for a video demo.*

1 pound trimmed, boneless, skinless chicken breasts (preferably free range)

1 teaspoon olive oil

1 teaspoon salt free garlic and herb bread seasoning

⅛ teaspoon plus ¹⁄₁₆ teaspoon sea salt

Olive oil spray (propellant free)

1 cup white onion slivers

4 (¾ ounce) slices reduced fat provolone cheese (preferably natural)

8 small iceberg lettuce leaves

3 tablespoons (1 ¼ ounces) drained, jarred, sliced pickled hot or sweet cherry peppers, or less to taste

4 tablespoons low sodium or no salt added ketchup

1 Shave the chicken by holding a very sharp knife at a 45 degree angle and cutting slivers from the breast, basically tearing it until it's all shaved—it should be cut much more finely than if it were simply sliced. Transfer the shaved chicken to a medium bowl. Drizzle the olive oil over top. Season with the seasoning and salt. Toss the mixture until the chicken is evenly seasoned.

2 Lightly mist a large nonstick frying pan with spray. Add the onions and place the pan over medium heat. Cook the onions until they are tender and lightly browned. Remove them from the pan and cover to keep them warm.

3 Turn the heat to medium high and remove the pan from the heat just long enough to mist the pan with spray. Then add the chicken to the pan. Using 2 spatulas, cook the chicken by pulling it apart to ensure even browning as the shavings cook. When no longer pink and lightly browned on the outsides, turn off the heat and add the onions back to the pan. Quickly toss the onions and chicken and then spread the mixture in an even layer in the pan and top it with the cheese slices, side by side, so the cheese melts (if it's not melting from residual heat, turn the pan to low and place a lid over top just long enough to melt the cheese; you don't want the chicken to become dry).

4 When the cheese is melted, divide the chicken mixture evenly among the lettuce leaves (about ½ cup in each), placing it in the center of each leaf. Season with pepper or additional salt free seasoning, if desired. Top with the cherry peppers. Drizzle the ketchup evenly over each or serve it on the side. Enjoy immediately.

CHOICES/EXCHANGES
½ carbohydrate, 4 lean protein

PER SERVING
230 calories, 7 g fat, 3.2 g saturated fat, 0 g trans fat, 75 mg cholesterol, 330 mg sodium, 390 mg potassium, 10 g carbohydrate, 1 g fiber, 7 g sugars, 30 g protein, 300 mg phosphorus

PULLED CHICKEN TACOS WITH PAPAYA SLAW

Pulled Chicken Tacos with Papaya Slaw

1 tablespoon whole grain oat flour

¼ teaspoon garlic powder

⅛ teaspoon salt

Pinch freshly ground black pepper

1 pound trimmed, boneless, skinless chicken breasts (preferably free range), cut into 1 ½ inch cubes

½ tablespoon extra virgin olive oil

⅔ cup orange juice (not from concentrate)

⅔ cup apple cider vinegar

2 tablespoons all natural applewood flavored liquid smoke

8 taco sized (6 inches in diameter) corn tortillas (preferably made with only corn, lime, and salt)

2 ⅔ cups Sweet Papaya Slaw (see page 149), divided

4 teaspoons sriracha (preferably natural), divided

1 handful fresh cilantro leaves, or to taste

*If you have the Sweet Papaya Slaw prepared.

1 In a medium resealable plastic bag, combine the flour, garlic powder, salt, and pepper. Add the chicken and shake the bag until the chicken is coated. Refrigerate the chicken for at least 15 minutes.

2 Preheat a medium nonstick soup pot over medium high heat. When it's hot, add the oil, then the chicken. Brown the chicken, about 1 minute per side, then turn the heat to medium and add the orange juice, vinegar, and liquid smoke.

3 When the liquid comes to a boil, reduce the heat to low (the liquid should still be boiling slightly). Cover and simmer the chicken, stirring occasionally, for 30–40 minutes or until it's very tender (the liquid will absorb into the meat and the pieces should be so tender they fall apart when smashed with a fork).

4 Using a slotted spoon, transfer the chicken (along with a bit of the liquid) to a medium mixing bowl. Using your fingers, 2 forks, or a pastry blender, separate the chicken pieces until the chicken is shredded.

5 During the last 15 minutes of cooking, stack the tortillas and wrap the stack in foil so it's completely covered. Heat them in a preheated 350°F oven until just warmed.

6 Place the tortillas side by side on a serving platter or place 2 tortillas side by side on each of 4 plates. Divide the meat evenly among the tortillas, laying it in a strip across the center one third of each tortilla. Top the chicken on each tortilla with ⅓ cup slaw. Drizzle ½ teaspoon sriracha (or up to 1 teaspoon, if desired) over the top of each. Then top each evenly with cilantro leaves. Fold the tacos and enjoy immediately.

recipe continued on next page »

Cook's Notes

Can't find whole grain oat flour? Don't worry. You can make your own by adding old fashioned oats to a food processor. Run it for a couple of minutes on high until the oats are as fine as flour! Need more helpful chef secrets and hacks? Visit me at **www. devinalexander.com/diabetes** where I'll share my secrets and give you the 411 on the specific brands I'm currently using.

When you buy corn tortillas, try to find some that have only corn, lime, and salt on the ingredient list—and make sure they don't have a lot of salt. Many brands have tons of chemicals and additives, and they don't even taste better!

Make sure you compare brands when you buy your sriracha. There are natural varieties that are very low in salt and have virtually no sugar. But that is not the case with every product! If you like spicy foods, you can use up to 8 teaspoons of sriracha in this dish to add even more kick.

CHOICES/EXCHANGES
2 starch, 1 nonstarchy vegetable,
3 lean protein

PER SERVING
320 calories, 7 g fat, 1 g saturated fat, 0 g trans fat, 70 mg cholesterol, 500 mg sodium, 600 mg potassium, 34 g carbohydrate, 5 g fiber, 9 g sugars, 30 g protein, 255 mg phosphorus

Maple Chili Glazed Pork Tenderloin

People often overcook pork for fear that they'll get sick if it's undercooked. To solve this dilemma, I strongly suggest you invest in a meat thermometer. I'll happily suggest a brand and even show you exactly how to use it! Why spend good money on a pork tenderloin for a delicious recipe like this one and then not have it come out as amazingly well as it would in a restaurant? Visit me at **www.devinalexander.com/diabetes** *to learn some of my chef secrets, brand recommendations, and quick tutorials.*

1 (1 ¼ pound) trimmed pork tenderloin

1 teaspoon extra virgin olive oil

½ teaspoon Chinese five spice powder

⅛ teaspoon sea salt

1 tablespoon pure maple syrup

1 tablespoon chili garlic sauce (preferably natural)

1 Preheat the oven to 350°F.

2 Rub the pork tenderloin evenly with the olive oil. Then rub the Chinese five spice powder and salt evenly over it. Cover the tenderloin loosely with plastic wrap and let it stand for 15 minutes (if one end of the tenderloin is much thinner than the other, tuck it under to create a similar thickness throughout—this helps with even cooking).

3 Meanwhile, in a small bowl, whisk together the maple syrup and chili garlic sauce. Pour half of the mixture into a second bowl.

4 Heat a large nonstick, ovenproof frying pan over medium high heat. When the pan is hot, cook the tenderloin until it is just browned all over, about 1–2 minutes per surface. Then, using a pastry or basting brush (or carefully using your fingers if you don't have a pastry brush), evenly coat the tenderloin with half of the maple syrup mixture. Transfer the pan to the oven and cook the tenderloin uncovered until it is just barely pink inside or a meat thermometer inserted into the pork reaches 150°F, about 14–18 minutes.

5 Remove the pan from the oven and immediately place a sheet of foil loosely over the tenderloin (not over the whole pan). Allow it to sit for 5 minutes while the juices redistribute. Transfer the tenderloin to a cutting board. Add any pan drippings to the bowl with the remaining maple syrup mixture.

6 Holding your knife at a 45 degree angle, slice the pork into thin slices. Transfer it to a serving platter. Pour the remaining maple syrup mixture over top. Enjoy immediately.

Cook's Notes

Many brands of chili garlic sauce have a ton of sodium. If you use one that is high in sodium, you will not need to add much salt directly to the tenderloin so you may not use the whole ⅛ teaspoon. If you happen to find a sauce that is low in sodium, the roast will need additional salt, up to the full ⅛ teaspoon.

CHOICES/EXCHANGES
½ carbohydrate, 3 lean protein

PER SERVING
180 calories, 5 g fat, 1.4 g saturated fat, 0 g trans fat, 75 mg cholesterol, 200 mg sodium, 450 mg potassium, 5 g carbohydrate, 0 g fiber, 4 g sugars, 27 g protein, 245 mg phosphorus

Sweet & Spicy Pomegranate Pork Tenderloin

1 tablespoon pomegranate molasses

½ tablespoon stevia honey blend sweetener (such as Truvia Nectar)

½ teaspoon dried red pepper flakes

1 teaspoon extra virgin olive oil

1 (1 ¼ pound) pork tenderloin, trimmed (1 pound after being trimmed)

¼ teaspoon sea salt

Freshly ground black pepper, to taste

⅛ teaspoon garlic powder

Olive oil spray (propellant free)

Cook's Notes

Make sure to purchase a pomegranate molasses that is a pure pomegranate concentrate. Some are basically sugar water (if sugar is the first ingredient, definitely run!) with a bit of pomegranate flavor. Want to know which brands I use? I'm happy to share—just pop over to www.devinalexander.com/diabetes where I've set up a whole section of my website to provide info to help you get the most out of this book!

1 Preheat the oven to 350°F. Line a medium baking sheet with nonstick foil.

2 Add the molasses, sweetener, and red pepper flakes to a small bowl. Using a small whisk, stir them together until mixed well. Set aside.

3 Drizzle the olive oil evenly over the trimmed tenderloin. Using a pastry brush or your hands, rub it over the tenderloin to completely cover it. Then sprinkle the salt, pepper, and garlic powder evenly over it. If the tenderloin tapers at one end, tuck that end under just enough that it becomes the thickness of the rest of the tenderloin (this helps with even cooking).

4 Heat a large nonstick skillet to medium high heat. When the pan is hot, remove it from the heat just long enough to mist it with spray. Add the tenderloin. Cook it until it is just browned all over, about 1 minute per face.

5 Transfer the tenderloin to the prepared baking sheet. Using a small pastry brush, brush the pomegranate mixture on the top and sides of the tenderloin. Bake for 16–20 minutes or until the tenderloin is barely pink inside.

6 Remove the baking sheet from the oven and tent the pork loosely with aluminum foil for 5–10 minutes. Transfer the tenderloin to a cutting board, reserving any leftover *jus* (pan juices). Slice the pork at a diagonal into thin slices. Transfer it to a serving platter or divide the slices among 4 plates. Drizzle the remaining *jus* evenly over the slices. Serve immediately.

CHOICES/EXCHANGES
½ carbohydrate, 3 lean protein

PER SERVING
160 calories, 3.5 g fat, 1 g saturated fat, 0 g trans fat, 75 mg cholesterol, 210 mg sodium, 460 mg potassium, 5 g carbohydrate, 0 g fiber, 4 g sugars, 24 g protein, 280 mg phosphorus

SWEET & SPICY POMEGRANATE PORK TENDERLOIN

Grilled Ahi with Olive Tomato Tapenade

I have an amazing team member in my office right now. Amy started as a social media intern, and she'd never cooked a meal in her life. She's a brilliant woman. One day I was stuck for a recipe tester when I was on deadline for an article I was writing for Muscle & Fitness *magazine so I asked her to give it a try. She was great! (I truly believe that anyone can cook—if you find the right recipes and follow them!) This recipe was the third dish Amy ever cooked, and she was hooked; she couldn't believe how easy it was. In honor of her, I did a twist on the recipe to make it friendly for everyone, not only bodybuilders. I hope, no matter your level of cooking skill, you enjoy this dish as much as Amy and I do!*

½ medium Roma or plum tomato (about 2 ounces), cut into ¼ inch cubes

1 tablespoon plus 2 teaspoons black olive tapenade

1 (4 ounce) sashimi grade ahi tuna steak

Olive oil spray (propellant free)

1/32 teaspoon sea salt

Freshly ground black pepper, to taste

1 Preheat a grill to high.

2 Mix the tomatoes and the tapenade in a small bowl.

3 Lightly mist both sides of the tuna steak with spray then season both sides with the salt and pepper. Grill it just until the outside is grilled (this dish is meant to be made sushi style), about 45–90 seconds. Flip the steak and repeat on the other side. Carefully (without burning yourself) sear the edges in same fashion, if desired.

4 Transfer the tuna to a serving plate. Top it with the tapenade mixture. Enjoy immediately.

Cook's Notes

Look for a black olive tapenade that is relatively low in fat and calories. The one I use has 4 g of fat per 2 tablespoon serving.

CHOICES/EXCHANGES
4 lean protein

PER SERVING
190 calories, 5 g fat, 1.1 g saturated fat, 0 g trans fat, 45 mg cholesterol, 380 mg sodium, 620 mg potassium, 4 g carbohydrate, 1 g fiber, 3 g sugars, 27 g protein, 320 mg phosphorus

Bacon Confetti Topped Scallops

8 ounces sea scallops (about 10 large scallops)

¹⁄₁₆ teaspoon sea salt

Freshly ground black pepper, to taste

Olive oil spray (propellant free)

¼ teaspoon freshly minced garlic

2 slices center cut bacon (preferably nitrate free)

½ tablespoon freshly minced chives

Cook's Notes

Use a pan big enough that all the scallops can be placed in a single layer without touching each other.

Make sure that the bacon is crispy. If it's not completely cooked, you won't get the indulgent bacon taste and awesome texture that complements the scallops so well!

1 Gently pat the scallops with a paper towel to remove any excess moisture. Season them all over with the salt and pepper.

2 Mist a medium nonstick frying pan with spray. Place it over medium heat. Add the garlic. Cook it, stirring frequently, until it is tender and just starting to brown. Remove the garlic to a bowl and add the bacon to the pan. Cook the bacon until it is crisp, about 1–3 minutes per side on a gas burner (longer on an electric burner). Transfer the bacon to a paper towel–lined plate and cover it with a pot lid or foil to keep it warm.

3 Turn the heat to medium high. When the bacon fat is hot enough that it sizzles when you add a scallop, add the scallops (if you put one in and it does not sizzle, carefully remove it, wait a few seconds, and try again; be careful not to burn yourself). Cook the scallops until they are browned (but not burned), then flip them and cook them until they brown on the other side, about 1–3 minutes per side. They'll likely be cooked by this point. If they are still translucent in the centers, turn the heat to low and continue cooking until they are cooked through.

4 Chop the bacon into fine pieces and mix it with the cooked garlic. Divide the scallops between 2 serving plates and arrange them so the scallops are touching each other. Top them evenly with the bacon and garlic then the chives. Enjoy immediately.

CHOICES/EXCHANGES
3 lean protein

PER SERVING
120 calories, 3 g fat, 1 g saturated fat, 0 g trans fat, 45 mg cholesterol, 380 mg sodium, 365 mg potassium, 3 g carbohydrate, 0 g fiber, 0 g sugars, 21 g protein, 250 mg phosphorus

Wasabi Crusted Salmon

1 ounce natural baked wasabi seasoned crispy green pea snacks (or roasted broad beans)

1–2 teaspoons prepared wasabi

2 (4 ounce) skinless salmon fillets (preferably wild caught)

Cook's Notes

Roasted broad beans and roasted peas have become increasingly available on the market. They seemed to emerge first in natural foods stores and then got picked up by major grocery chains...and I couldn't be happier! They're crunchy (baked, not fried!) and can be delicious as a snack on their own. They're also a great way to add a little "fried" crunch to a dish without adding something that's really fried. Buy the roasted variety and find one that doesn't have any added sugar. I've seen many varieties that have no saturated fat, no added sugar, and are low in sodium. Every once in a while, I have seen cane sugar added to one of these products. It's not a lot, but hey, who needs it?

You can find wasabi in the international section of your grocery store near the soy sauce.

1 Preheat the oven to 400°F. Line a small baking sheet with nonstick foil.

2 Add the crispy peas or beans to a resealable plastic bag. Using the flat side of a meat mallet or a rolling pin, crush them so that some pieces are finely chopped and others are near whole.

3 Spoon the wasabi into a small bowl.

4 Place the salmon fillets side by side with a bit of room in between them on a dinner plate. Using a pastry brush (or a spoon or knife), brush the wasabi evenly over the sides and tops of the fillets (if you like a wasabi kick, you can use 2 teaspoons of wasabi; if not, stick with 1 teaspoon). Sprinkle the crushed peas or beans over the top of the fillets.

5 Transfer the salmon fillets to the prepared baking sheet so they do not touch. Press and/or sprinkle any crumbs that remain on the plate into/onto the top of the salmon, dividing them evenly between the fillets. Bake the salmon until it reaches desired doneness (somewhere between just barely and no longer translucent), about 6–10 minutes. Enjoy immediately.

CHOICES/EXCHANGES
½ carbohydrate, 3 lean protein, 1 ½ fat

PER SERVING
240 calories, 11 g fat, 2.7 g saturated fat, 0 g trans fat, 60 mg cholesterol, 160 mg sodium, 400 mg potassium, 10 g carbohydrate, 0 g fiber, 3 g sugars, 24 g protein, 290 mg phosphorus

Bruschetta Plank Salmon

I can't emphasize enough how very important it is to soak your wooden plank before you put it on a grill when making this recipe. I once made this dish for a Biggest Loser Reunion Party I hosted in my kitchen before a finale for all of the former contestants. I needed to cook so much salmon that my plank, which had been soaking for hours, started to catch fire. I quickly learned that I needed multiple planks to cook that much salmon. But please don't let that story dissuade you! I cook on planks all the time and wouldn't trade it for the world; you get pure delicious flavor infusion with zero calories!

1 wooden grill plank

2 (4 ounce) salmon fillets

Olive oil spray (propellant free)

⅛ teaspoon sea salt

Freshly ground black pepper, to taste

4 tablespoons Body Lovin' Bruschetta (see page 188)

*If you have the Body Lovin' Bruschetta prepared.

1 Soak the plank in water for at least 1 hour (or overnight).

2 Preheat a grill to medium.

3 Lightly mist the salmon fillets with the spray, then season them with salt and pepper.

4 Place the plank on the grill for 15 seconds, or just until it has dried (watch it carefully so it doesn't burn or catch fire). Place the salmon fillets, side by side and not touching, on the plank. Grill them for about 4–6 minutes until they are just barely translucent inside, making sure to check on them every minute or so to make sure the plank isn't burning.

5 Transfer the fillets to serving plates and divide the bruschetta evenly between them (2 tablespoons on each), spooning it over the center one third of each fillet. Serve immediately.

Cook's Notes

When purchasing salmon, do your best to buy the thick part of the salmon (the tail end is used to swim, so it's tougher). And ask the fishmonger to remove the skin for you if it's not already removed.

CHOICES/EXCHANGES
3 lean protein, 1 fat

PER SERVING
190 calories, 9 g fat, 1 g saturated fat, 0 trans fat, 60 mg cholesterol, 270 mg sodium, 630 mg potassium, 2 g carbohydrate, 0 g fiber, 1 g sugars, 23 g protein, 235 mg phosphorus

Pan Fried Black Cod with Pink Grapefruit Salsa

2 (16 ounce) pink grapefruit

1 tablespoon freshly squeezed lime juice

1 tablespoon finely chopped red onion

2 tablespoons chopped fresh cilantro leaves

1 tablespoon finely chopped jalapeño pepper (seeded if you want a more mild heat)

⅛ teaspoon plus ⅛ teaspoon sea salt, divided

4 (4 ounce) black cod fillets, bones removed

2 teaspoons olive oil

Salt free Mexican seasoning, to taste

Cook's Notes

The grapefruit salsa needs to be made at least 2 hours before serving. But you can make it up to 2 days ahead of time.

1 Cut a slice off both ends of each grapefruit just thick enough to cut off the peel and pith (the white part). Place one grapefruit on a flat surface. Carefully following the natural curve of the grapefruit, cut away the peel and pith with a small paring knife, beginning at the top and ending at the bottom, until the entire grapefruit is peeled. Cut between the "skins" of the grapefruit to remove the grapefruit sections, trying to keep them as whole as possible. Add the sections to a small mixing bowl as you progress. Squeeze the remaining portion (the skins) of the grapefruit over the bowl to release any remaining juice into the bowl, then discard the skins. Repeat with the remaining grapefruit.

2 Add the lime juice, red onion, cilantro, jalapeño, and ⅛ teaspoon of salt to the bowl with the grapefruit sections. Using a rubber spatula, gently mix the ingredients together. Transfer the salsa to a resealable container with a lid and store it in the refrigerator for 2 hours (or up to 2 days).

3 Place the black cod fillets on a plate and drizzle the oil evenly over both sides. Rub them with your fingers to evenly disperse the oil. Season the fillets with the seasoning to taste and the remaining ⅛ teaspoon of salt.

4 Place a large nonstick frying pan over medium high heat. When the pan is hot, add the fillets. Cook them until the outsides are just lightly browned, 1–2 minutes per side. Then reduce the heat to medium and cook until the fillets are no longer translucent throughout, about 1–4 minutes per side depending on thickness. Transfer each fillet to a plate. Top each with one quarter of the salsa (about ½ cup on each). Enjoy immediately.

CHOICES/EXCHANGES
½ fruit, 3 medium-fat protein, 1 fat

PER SERVING
290 calories, 20 g fat, 4.1 g saturated fat, 0 g trans fat, 60 mg cholesterol, 200 mg sodium, 560 mg potassium, 10 g carbohydrate, 1 g fiber, 6 g sugars, 17 g protein, 215 mg phosphorus

Quick Shrimp Tacos

1 cup finely shredded cabbage

2 tablespoons yogurt based creamy Mexican or Southwest bottled salad dressing

½ teaspoon olive oil

½ teaspoon salt free Mexican seasoning

4 ounces large shrimp (preferably wild caught), peeled and deveined

2 (6 inch) corn tortillas (preferably made with only corn, lime, and salt)

½ tablespoon taco sauce (preferably natural)

A few cilantro leaves, to taste

Lime wedges, for squeezing

1 Preheat a grill to medium.

2 In a small bowl, toss together the cabbage and dressing until well combined and set aside.

3 In another small bowl, mix together the oil, seasoning, and shrimp until well combined. Grill the shrimp 1–2 minutes per side, or until the shrimp are pink and fully opaque throughout.

4 Warm the tortillas on the grill, about 30 seconds to 1 minute (just until warm, you don't want them to crisp).

5 Add the tortillas to a plate and divide the cabbage mixture evenly between the tortillas, spooning it down the center one third of each tortilla. Top each tortilla with half of the shrimp. Drizzle the taco sauce over each taco and add the cilantro leaves. Serve with lime wedges on the side for squeezing. Enjoy immediately.

Cook's Notes

I love some of the yogurt based salad dressings that have been popping up in recent years. Be careful, however, when selecting a dressing for this recipe; some have as much as 300 mg of sodium for only a couple of tablespoons. Want to know which dressings I'm using? Visit me at **www.devinalexander.com/diabetes** where I share tons of the brands I'm using along with chef secrets and so much more.

I enjoy heating my tortillas on the grill because you can get beautiful grill marks. That being said, they'll burn quickly on the grill. So if you don't want to watch them super closely, wrap them in foil so they are covered completely and put them on the grill for a couple of minutes. The foil packet will keep them nice and hot for a few minutes after grilling too!

CHOICES/EXCHANGES
1 ½ starch, 1 nonstarchy vegetable, 3 lean protein, 1 fat

PER SERVING
330 calories, 9 g fat, 1.5 g saturated fat, 0 g trans fat, 175 mg cholesterol, 440 mg sodium, 425 mg potassium, 32 g carbohydrate, 5 g fiber, 5 g sugars, 28 g protein, 415 mg phosphorus

Tomato Feta Shrimp Pasta

Olive oil spray (propellant free)

¼ cup finely chopped sweet onion

1 tablespoon freshly minced garlic

1 tablespoon finely chopped fresh oregano leaves

1 can (14–14.5 ounces) no added salt Italian cherry tomatoes (Italian whole miniature tomatoes or tomatoes in tomato purée)

⅛ teaspoon reduced sodium salt substitute

Freshly ground black pepper, to taste

2 tablespoons finely chopped mint leaves

2 teaspoons extra virgin olive oil

8 ounces peeled and deveined extra large (21–25 count or larger) shrimp (preferably wild caught)

1 ounce (¼ cup) crumbled light feta cheese (preferably natural)

⅓ cup coarsely chopped flat leaf parsley leaves

4 ounces uncooked green lentil pasta or 3 ounces high fiber whole grain rotini or penne

1 Preheat the oven to 450°F.

2 Place a large pot of water over high heat and bring it to a boil.

3 Lightly mist a medium ovenproof (to 450°F) frying pan with spray. Place it over medium heat. Add the onion, garlic, and oregano. Cook them, stirring occasionally with a wooden spoon, just until they become fragrant, about 2–3 minutes. Stir in the tomatoes, salt substitute, and pepper, and turn the heat to medium high. Continue cooking and stirring the tomatoes constantly until they become jam like, about 5–7 minutes (if you don't continue stirring them, the sauce could burn and some will boil away).

4 Turn off the heat and stir in the mint, olive oil, and shrimp. Make sure the shrimp are in a single layer and are covered by the sauce as much as possible. Sprinkle the cheese and parsley over top. Transfer the pan to the oven and bake the shrimp until the shrimp in the center of the pan have plumped and are no longer translucent in the center and the cheese is melty, about 8–14 minutes.

5 Meanwhile, cook the pasta in the large pot of boiling water according to the package directions, omitting any butter or oil. Divide the pasta between 2 serving bowls. Spoon half of the shrimp mixture (about 1 cup) over each bowl of pasta. Enjoy immediately.

Cook's Notes

I buy canned Italian cherry tomatoes for recipes like this one, and they are so worth the extra money, especially when health concerns are involved. They have no added sugars but are so sweet and they tend to be much lower in sodium. Our American tomatoes don't tend to be as sweet and our canned tomatoes often have additives and preservatives.

A lot of people don't realize it, but there is a difference between reduced fat, light, and low fat products. The term "reduced fat" means that a product contains at least 25% less fat than the original product. If a label says "light" it means the food contains 50% less fat than the original. But these terms are tricky because you don't know the amount of fat they're being compared to. It's possible that a "reduced fat" product could actually be lower in fat than a "light" product. "Low fat," on the other hand, always means that a product has 3 g of fat or less per serving. I tend to avoid most fat free products because they often have chemicals and ingredients I don't want to consume (the exception to this rule is when it comes to milk, quark, and yogurts—those are often natural even when fat free). The moral of the story is to always read the labels.

I generally make this dish with green lentil pasta to make it extra nutritious. If you use lentil pasta, I strongly recommend you don't cook the pasta as long as the package says to cook it. If you cook it past al dente, it starts to get mushy and sort of tastes like beans. Otherwise this yummy sauce masks the bean taste.

CHOICES/EXCHANGES
2 ½ starch, 2 nonstarchy vegetable, 4 lean protein

PER SERVING
430 calories, 8 g fat, 2 g saturated fat, 0 g trans fat, 195 mg cholesterol, 480 mg sodium, 1620 mg potassium, 50 g carbohydrate, 11 g fiber, 9 g sugars, 43 g protein, 530 mg phosphorus

CHEESY LASAGNA ROLLUPS

Cheesy Lasagna Rollups

Being Italian, there is no way that I can live without some sort of lasagna! I just can't. Here's a version of lasagna that is not only delicious, but very satisfying! Be sure you squeeze the heck out of the kale; if you remove the liquid, you can barely taste it.

Olive oil spray (propellant free)

½ teaspoon extra virgin olive oil

8 whole wheat or fiber enriched lasagna noodles

6 ounces baby kale leaves (remove any coarse stems before weighing)

1 ½ cups fat free ricotta cheese

1 egg white (preferably cage free)

2 tablespoons chopped parsley leaves

½ teaspoon garlic powder

2 teaspoons plus 1 tablespoon finely grated Parmesan cheese (preferably natural), divided

2 cups marinara sauce

2 ounces reduced fat mozzarella cheese

Fresh basil leaves, to taste, stems removed and cut into ribbons

1 Preheat the oven to 350°F. Lightly mist an 11 × 7 inch casserole or baking dish with spray.

2 Fill a large soup pot two thirds full with water. Place it over high heat. When the water has come to a boil, add the olive oil and noodles. Cook them until they are al dente (tender with a slight bite), about 6–8 minutes, stirring occasionally. Drain the noodles (don't rinse them) and carefully (being sure not to burn yourself) place them on a large sheet of waxed paper or parchment paper so they don't touch.

3 Place a large nonstick frying pan over medium heat. Add the kale. Place a medium lid (one that is smaller than the pan) directly onto the kale. When the kale on the bottom is wilted, lift the lid. Using a wooden spoon, stir the kale and then cover it again. Repeat until all the kale has wilted, about 2–5 minutes. Remove the kale from the heat and let it cool completely.

4 Meanwhile, in a medium mixing bowl, combine the ricotta, egg white, parsley, garlic powder, and 2 teaspoons of the Parmesan. Mix them until well combined. Set aside.

5 Squeeze as much water out of the cooled kale as possible. Then transfer it to a lint free kitchen towel and twist it until all the liquid has been removed. It should be dry. Transfer it to a cutting board and roughly chop it until it's finely chopped. Add the chopped kale to the ricotta mixture. Using a rubber spatula, mix the kale and ricotta until well combined.

recipe continued on next page »

Cheesy Lasagna Rollups continued from previous page »

6 Lay the noodles on a cutting board or other clean work surface side by side so that one of the shorter ends of each noodle is closest to you. Divide the ricotta mixture among the noodles, about ¼ cup in each, spreading it over the entire length of the noodles except the last inch on the side furthest from you. Roll each noodle, starting at the end closest to you, being careful to keep the filling inside.

7 Spread 1 cup of the marinara sauce on the bottom of the prepared casserole dish. Add the lasagna rolls side by side, evenly spaced in the dish. Drizzle the remaining sauce over the tops so some stays on top and the rest drips down to cover the rollups as much as possible. Distribute the mozzarella evenly over the top. Then sprinkle the remaining tablespoon of Parmesan evenly over top. Cover the baking dish with nonstick foil (shiny side up), and bake the rollups for 30 minutes.

8 Remove the foil. Bake the rollups uncovered until cheese has melted and has started to become just golden brown in spots, about 5 minutes. Garnish with fresh basil ribbons, if desired. Enjoy immediately.

Cook's Notes

Look for a natural marinara sauce that has less than 200 mg of sodium and no added sugar.

CHOICES/EXCHANGES
2 ½ starch, 1 nonstarchy vegetable,
2 lean protein, ½ fat

PER SERVING
340 calories, 7 g fat, 1.5 g saturated fat, 0 g trans fat, 40 mg cholesterol, 450 mg sodium, 750 mg potassium, 45 g carbohydrate, 9 g fiber, 8 g sugars, 25 g protein, 445 mg phosphorus

Skinny Skampi

Whatever you do, when you start preparing this recipe, make sure you have all of your ingredients measured and ready to go before adding the wine and lemon juice to the pan. Though it's always recommended that you prep everything in advance, it's not always essential. It's especially important for this recipe, however, because the wine and lemon juice will evaporate while you're off measuring other ingredients. Not only could this be detrimental to the taste, but you could easily burn your pan.

Also, notice that the shrimp are cooked in batches. It's important not to cut corners on that. Overcrowding the pan will not yield the same better-than-at-your-local-restaurant results.

1 ¼ pounds large (26–30 count) shrimp (preferably wild caught), peeled (tails left on) and deveined

1 teaspoon extra virgin olive oil

¼ teaspoon salt

Freshly ground black pepper, to taste

Olive oil spray (propellant free)

6 cloves garlic, peeled and minced (about 2 ½ tablespoons)

¼ cup dry white wine

2 tablespoons fresh lemon juice

2 tablespoons light butter (stick, not tub)

1 tablespoon plus 1 tablespoon freshly minced parsley, divided

Cook's Notes

Don't know how to peel and devein shrimp? Visit **www.devinalexander.com/diabetes** and I'll show you how in a quick video.

1 Toss the shrimp with the olive oil, salt, and pepper in a medium bowl.

2 Lightly mist a large nonstick frying pan with spray. Place it over medium heat and add the garlic. Cook the garlic until it is just tender, about 5 minutes.

3 Remove the garlic from the pan. Turn the heat to high. When the skillet is hot, add half of the shrimp. When shrimp are lightly browned on one side, after about 1 minute (or less), flip them. Continue cooking the shrimp until they are just lightly browned and cooked through, about 1–3 minutes. Transfer the shrimp to a platter and cover it to keep them hot. Repeat with the remaining shrimp. Add them to the platter and cover.

4 Immediately add the wine and lemon juice to the pan. When the liquid is reduced by half, after about 30 seconds to 2 minutes, turn the heat to low (or off if the pan is hot enough to melt the butter without heat) and add the butter, the cooked garlic, and 1 tablespoon of the parsley. Use a wooden spoon or spatula to stir it until the butter is melted completely, about 30 seconds to 1 minute.

5 Spoon the sauce over the shrimp and toss well, then garnish with the remaining parsley. Enjoy immediately.

CHOICES/EXCHANGES
4 lean protein

PER SERVING
180 calories, 4 g fat, 1.2 g saturated fat, 0 g trans fat, 240 mg cholesterol, 330 mg sodium, 370 mg potassium, 3 g carbohydrate, 0 g fiber, 0 g sugars, 30 g protein, 310 mg phosphorus

SUPERIOR
Sides

Seasoned Curly Fries

*Curly fries are really easy and fun to make. The tool I use to cut the curly fries is called a twin curl cutter or twin curler and can be easily ordered online or found at kitchen stores or restaurant supply stores for just a few dollars. Don't know where to buy it or how to use it? Visit me at **www.devinalexander.com/diabetes** and I'll show you.*

4 russet potatoes (about 8 ounces each; 2 pounds total), peeled

1 teaspoon olive oil

1 teaspoon salt free garlic and herb bread seasoning

⅛ teaspoon sea salt

Olive oil spray (propellant free)

Twin curl cutter

1 Preheat the oven to 450°F. Line a small nonstick baking sheet with nonstick foil.

2 With a twin curl cutter, cut 12 ounces of potato curls, about 2 ⅔ cups, from the potatoes (cover the remaining potato scraps with water and refrigerate them to use in another recipe). Place the curls in a bowl and drizzle the olive oil over top. Then sprinkle the seasoning and salt over top. Toss the curls until they are evenly covered.

3 Arrange the curls, not touching, in a single layer on the prepared baking sheet. Bake them for 15 minutes. Rotate them and cook until lightly crisped on the outsides and tender throughout, about an additional 10–15 minutes. Lightly mist the finished fries with the spray. Enjoy immediately.

Cook's Notes

Make sure your curls are dry before cooking (blot them with a lint free towel or paper towels if necessary) to ensure they crisp on the outside. Note that when you use a twin curl cutter, you will need to unravel the pair of fries from each other before cooking.

CHOICES/EXCHANGES
2 starch

PER SERVING
150 calories, 2.5 g fat, 0.3 g saturated fat, 0 g trans fat, 0 mg cholesterol, 150 mg sodium, 920 mg potassium, 30 g carbohydrate, 3 g fiber, 3 g sugars, 3 g protein, 80 mg phosphorus

SEASONED CURLY FRIES

Battered Fries

Olive oil spray (propellant free)

¼ cup plus 1 teaspoon egg substitute

¼ cup whole grain oat flour

2 teaspoons ground paprika

¼ teaspoon cayenne pepper

¼ teaspoon onion powder

⅛ teaspoon garlic powder

⅛ teaspoon reduced sodium salt substitute

⅛ teaspoon plus ⅛ teaspoon sea salt, divided

1 ½ pounds light fleshed sweet potatoes (not all will be used for this recipe)

Crinkle cutter

1 Preheat the oven to 350°F. Line a large baking sheet with nonstick foil. Lightly mist it with spray.

2 In a medium mixing bowl, using a whisk for ease, mix the egg substitute, flour, paprika, cayenne, onion powder, garlic powder, salt substitute, and ⅛ teaspoon of salt.

3 Using a crinkle cutter, cut most of the peels from the potatoes. Discard the peels. Then, cut ½ inch thick by 4 inch long pieces until you have 1 pound of "fries" (about 3 ½ cups; reserve any remaining potato for another recipe). Transfer the fries to the mixing bowl with the batter. Gently toss them until they are evenly coated. Place them on the prepared baking sheet so they don't touch. Lightly mist them with spray.

4 Bake the fries for 20 minutes, then flip them and continue baking them until the fries are golden brown and are cooked through, about an additional 12–18 minutes. Mist them lightly with spray. Sprinkle the remaining ⅛ teaspoon of salt over top. Enjoy immediately.

Cook's Notes

If you're following a gluten free diet, make sure the oat flour you use is gluten free!

CHOICES/EXCHANGES
2 starch

PER SERVING
130 calories, 1 g fat, 0 g saturated fat, 0 g trans fat, 0 mg cholesterol, 240 mg sodium, 500 mg potassium, 27 g carbohydrate, 4 g fiber, 5 g sugars, 5 g protein, 75 mg phosphorus

Sea Salt Dusted Crinkle Cuts

You'll need a crinkle cutting tool for this recipe as well as several other recipes in this chapter. The good news is that crinkle cutters tend to cost only a few dollars. Want a little guidance on finding or purchasing a crinkle cutter or any other equipment within these pages? I'm happy to help! Go to www.devinalexander.com/diabetes for my tips and recommendations.

1 ½ pounds baking potatoes

1 ½ teaspoons extra virgin olive oil

¼ teaspoon plus ⅛ teaspoon sea salt, divided

Crinkle cutter

1 Preheat the oven to 400°F. Line a large baking sheet with nonstick foil.

2 Use a crinkle cutter to peel the potatoes by cutting close to the edges on each side. Discard the peels. Then use the crinkle cutter to cut the peeled potatoes into ⅓ inch thick "fries". After discarding the peels and any deformed cuts, you should have approximately 1 pound (about 4 cups) of fries. If you have more than 1 pound, store the extra in the refrigerator in water in an airtight container for use at a later time.

3 Toss the fries with the olive oil and ¼ teaspoon of the salt. Then place them in a single layer, not touching, on the prepared baking sheet. Bake them for 12 minutes. Flip them and continue baking until they are tender inside and done to your liking on the outsides, about another 12–15 minutes for softer fries or 16–20 minutes for crisper fries.

4 Toss them in the remaining salt. Enjoy immediately.

CHOICES/EXCHANGES
1 ½ starch

PER SERVING
100 calories, 2 g fat, 0.2 g saturated fat, 0 g trans fat, 0 mg cholesterol, 210 mg sodium, 610 mg potassium, 20 g carbohydrate, 2 g fiber, 2 g sugars, 2 g protein, 50 mg phosphorus

PARMESAN GARLIC SQUASH "FRIES"

Parmesan Garlic Squash "Fries"

Make this recipe for people who don't think they like squash, just don't tell them that these are squash fries. Call them "Garlic Parmesan Fries" instead—soon they'll swear by them!

Olive oil spray (propellant free)

1 butternut squash (at least 2 ½ pounds; not all will be used for this recipe) or 1 pound crinkle cut butternut squash sticks

2 teaspoons extra virgin olive oil

¼ cup shredded Parmesan cheese (preferably natural)

¼ cup finely chopped flat leaf parsley

2 tablespoons freshly minced garlic

½ teaspoon ground paprika

⅛ teaspoon sea salt

Crinkle cutter

1 Preheat the oven to 325°F. Line a large baking sheet with nonstick foil. Lightly mist it with spray.

2 Cut both ends from the squash, then peel it, making sure to remove both the very outer layer of peel and the inner bit that is much lighter than most of the squash. Cut the squash in half lengthwise. Using a large spoon, scrape out the seeds. Cut the top portions just above the seeds off both halves (reserve the area with the seeds for another recipe). Using a crinkle cutter, cut ½ inch thick by approximately 4 inch long fry like pieces from the top portions until you have 1 pound of "fries" (reserve any excess with the bottoms).

3 Transfer the fries to a medium mixing bowl. Drizzle them with olive oil then sprinkle the cheese, parsley, garlic, paprika, and salt over top. Gently toss them until the fries are evenly coated.

4 Place the fries on the prepared baking sheet so they don't touch. Bake them until the fries are caramelized and tender throughout, about 20–25 minutes per side. Enjoy immediately.

Cook's Notes

This recipe calls for a squash that is at least 2 ½ pounds so you can handle it with ease. You will have a hearty portion of the squash leftover to use in another recipe. But if you buy a smaller squash, it will be very difficult to get even, fry like pieces.

CHOICES/EXCHANGES
1 starch, ½ fat

PER SERVING
110 calories, 4 g fat, 1 g saturated fat, 0 g trans fat, 5 mg cholesterol, 190 mg sodium, 435 mg potassium, 15 g carbohydrate, 3 g fiber, 3 g sugars, 4 g protein, 45 mg phosphorus

Thyme-ly Butternut Squash "Fries"

Olive oil spray (propellant free)

1 medium butternut squash
(at least 2 ½ pounds) OR
1 pound crinkle cut butternut
squash sticks

2 teaspoons extra virgin olive oil

¼ teaspoon plus ⅛ teaspoon sea
salt, divided

⅛ teaspoon reduced sodium
salt substitute

1 teaspoon freshly minced garlic

1 teaspoon fresh chopped
thyme leaves

Crinkle cutter

Cook's Notes

I love these "fries" when they are cooked until caramelized, about 50–55 minutes (depending on your oven). If you've never been a butternut squash fan (or if you cook for someone who isn't), you might find that by cooking these fries longer, you have a huge change of heart. When cooked that long, they'll take on a new flavor and yield about 1 ¾ cups of fries. If you like your fries a little less caramelized, they're perfectly done after around 35–40 minutes in the oven and will yield about 2 ⅓ cups.

1 Preheat the oven to 325°F. Line a small baking sheet with nonstick foil. Lightly mist it with spray.

2 Cut both ends from the squash, then peel it, making sure to remove both the very outer layer of peel and the inner bit that is much lighter than most of the squash. Cut the squash in half lengthwise. Using a large spoon, scrape out the seeds. Cut the top portions (just above the seeds) off both halves (reserve the area with the seeds for another recipe). Using a crinkle cutter, cut ½ inch thick by approximately 4 inch long "fries" from the top portion until you have 1 pound of "fries" (reserve any excess with the bottoms).

3 Transfer the fries to a medium mixing bowl. Drizzle the olive oil over them, then sprinkle ¼ teaspoon of salt and the salt substitute over top. Gently toss the fries until they are evenly coated. Place them on the prepared baking sheet so they don't touch. Bake them for 15 minutes, then flip them and continue baking for 15 minutes.

4 Add the garlic and thyme and gently "toss" the fries, then continue cooking them until they are golden brown on the outsides and very tender throughout— they should be very sweet with no crunch at all—about 4–10 additional minutes per side. Sprinkle the fries with the remaining ⅛ teaspoon of salt. Enjoy immediately.

CHOICES/EXCHANGES
1 starch

PER SERVING
70 calories, 2.5 g fat, 0.3 g saturated fat, 0 g trans fat, 0 mg cholesterol, 240 mg sodium, 450 mg potassium, 14 g carbohydrate, 2 g fiber, 2 g sugars, 1 g protein, 40 mg phosphorus

Rosemary Mashed Potatoes

I've served these yummy mashed potatoes at numerous Thanksgiving dinners and people always ask, "What did you do to the potatoes?" They taste so good but people can't quite figure out what they are. In many cases it's because people aren't familiar with light sweet potatoes. I use light sweet potatoes often for this exact reason—whether people like sweet potatoes or not, they tend to like these since they look (and taste) more like white potatoes.

1 ½ pounds peeled light fleshed sweet potatoes, cut into 1 inch cubes

3 tablespoons Greek yogurt cream cheese, room temperature

3 tablespoons fat free milk

1 tablespoon vegan butter (from a stick, not a tub), melted

¾ teaspoon finely chopped fresh rosemary leaves

½ teaspoon reduced sodium salt substitute

Pinch garlic powder

1 Fill a large soup pot halfway with cold water. Add the potatoes. Place the pot over high heat and bring the water to a boil. Cook the potatoes until they are tender when poked with a fork, about 12–15 minutes.

2 Meanwhile, using a hand mixer fitted with beaters, in a medium mixing bowl, beat the cream cheese until it is smooth. On low speed, beat in the milk until well combined.

3 Drain the cooked potatoes well and transfer them to the bowl with the cream cheese mixture. Beat in the potatoes, butter, rosemary, salt substitute, and garlic powder until combined (leaving some lumps). Enjoy immediately.

CHOICES/EXCHANGES
1 ½ starch

PER SERVING
120 calories, 3 g fat, 1 g saturated fat, 0 g trans fat, 3 mg cholesterol, 170 mg sodium, 410 mg potassium, 21 g carbohydrate, 3 g fiber, 8 g sugars, 3 g protein, 55 mg phosphorus

Chipotle Honey Sweet Potato Mash

These potatoes have a little bit of a kick, but they're not too spicy. My father and I are big fans of spicy foods. My mother, on the other hand, is not—but she loves these potatoes!

Never heard of Greek yogurt cream cheese or stevia honey blend? Want to know what brand of salt I'm using today? I'd love to tell you. Just pop over to www.devinalexander.com/diabetes. I've dedicated an entire section of my website to assisting you so you can get more out of this cookbook!

1 pound sweet potato cubes (peeled; 1 inch cubes)

3 tablespoons 100% orange juice (not from concentrate)

2 tablespoons Greek yogurt cream cheese, room temperature

2 teaspoons stevia honey blend sweetener (such as Truvia Nectar)

½ tablespoon chopped canned chipotle peppers in adobo sauce

¾ teaspoon reduced sodium salt substitute

Freshly ground black pepper, to taste

1 Add the sweet potatoes to a large pot of cold water and place over high heat. When the water comes to a boil, cook them for 12–15 minutes, or until the potatoes are very tender.

2 Drain the potatoes and add them to a medium mixing bowl along with the orange juice, cream cheese, sweetener, chipotles, and the salt substitute. With a hand mixer, beat the ingredients until smooth. Season with pepper. Serve immediately.

Cook's Notes

Be sure to cut the potatoes into relatively uniform pieces so they cook evenly.

Look for canned chipotle peppers in adobo near the Mexican chilies and enchilada sauce in your grocery store. Pull a pepper from the adobo sauce and chop it finely. Add ½ tablespoon of chopped peppers to the potatoes.

CHOICES/EXCHANGES
2 starch

PER SERVING
130 calories, 1 g fat, 0.5 g saturated fat, 0 g trans fat, 0 mg cholesterol, 220 mg sodium, 745 mg potassium, 27 g carbohydrate, 4 g fiber, 9 g sugars, 3 g protein, 55 mg phosphorus

Mediterranean Farro

If you've never had it before, farro is a nutty flavored ancient grain. I love adding it to salads and using it as the base of scrumptious side dishes like I do here.

¼ cup (about 2 ounces) cucumber, seeded (not peeled), cut into ¼ inch cubes

¼ cup (about 2 ounces) small red onion, cut into ¼ inch cubes

2 small cloves garlic, peeled, ends trimmed, and minced

⅓ cup flat leaf parsley leaves, finely chopped

2 (about 2 ½ ounces each) Roma (plum) tomatoes, seeded and cut into ¼ inch cubes

2 cups cooked farro

8 pitted Kalamata olives, finely chopped

1 ounce finely crumbled light feta cheese (preferably natural)

1 tablespoon freshly squeezed lemon juice

1 tablespoon good quality extra virgin olive oil

⅛ teaspoon sea salt

⅛ teaspoon reduced sodium salt substitute

*If you have the farro prepared.

1 Add the cucumber, onion, garlic, parsley, tomatoes, farro, olives, feta, lemon juice, and olive oil to a medium mixing bowl.

2 Season with the salt and salt substitute. Enjoy immediately or store in an airtight container for up to 1 day.

CHOICES/EXCHANGES
1 starch, 1 fat

PER SERVING
120 calories, 4 g fat, 1 g saturated fat, 0 g trans fat, 0 mg cholesterol, 220 mg sodium, 130 mg potassium, 16 g carbohydrate, 2 g fiber, 1 g sugars, 4 g protein, 90 mg phosphorus

Roasted Carrots with Creamy Carrot Top Pesto

You need to be sure to buy carrots with stems for this recipe (unless you already have the carrot top pesto made). It's best to scrub the carrots instead of peeling them for this recipe. Use a veggie brush or scrubber. If you're like me and love kitchen "toys," they make so many fun carrot (and other veggie) scrubbers. Want a peek into my kitchen? Visit me at www.devinalexander.com/diabetes for that and so much more!

1 pound trimmed, well scrubbed (unpeeled) heirloom carrots with tops or other carrots with tops (leave about 2 inches of stem on)

½ tablespoon extra virgin olive oil

1⁄16 teaspoon sea salt

Freshly ground black pepper, to taste

½ cup Creamy Carrot Top Pesto (see page 183)

*If you have the Creamy Carrot Top Pesto prepared.

1 Preheat the oven to 425°F. Line a medium baking sheet with nonstick foil.

2 In a large bowl, combine the carrots with the olive oil, salt, and pepper and toss them until they are evenly coated.

3 Place the carrots side by side on the prepared baking sheet. Bake them for 8 minutes. Then flip them and continue baking (roasting, really) until the carrots are lightly browned and tender with a bit of a "bite," or to your desired doneness, about 6–12 more minutes (cooking time will vary based on the size and even the color of the carrots used—yellow ones tend to take a bit longer than orange carrots of the same size).

4 Spoon the pesto over the center two thirds of a serving platter or spoon 2 tablespoons over the center two thirds of each of 4 side dish plates. Top the pesto with the carrots or one fourth of the carrots, respectively. Enjoy immediately.

CHOICES/EXCHANGES
2 nonstarchy vegetable, 1 fat

PER SERVING
110 calories, 6 g fat, 1 g saturated fat, 0 g trans fat, 0 mg cholesterol, 240 mg sodium, 410 mg potassium, 11 g carbohydrate, 3 g fiber, 6 g sugars, 4 g protein, 75 mg phosphorus

ROASTED CARROTS WITH CREAMY CARROT TOP PESTO

Orange Roasted Asparagus

1 ½ teaspoons extra virgin olive oil

½ pound trimmed asparagus

⅛ teaspoon sea salt

Freshly ground black pepper, to taste

1 tablespoon grated orange zest

1 large clove garlic, peeled, ends trimmed, and very finely chopped

1 Preheat the oven to 400°F. Line a baking sheet with nonstick foil.

2 In a large mixing bowl, drizzle the olive oil over the asparagus then toss the spears to evenly cover them. Lay the spears side by side on the prepared baking sheet. Sprinkle them with salt and pepper.

3 Bake them for 4–10 minutes (4 minutes for thin spears or 10 minutes for thick ones), then sprinkle the orange zest and garlic over them. Continue cooking until the spears are crisp tender, about 2–3 more minutes. Transfer the spears to a serving platter. Enjoy immediately.

Cook's Notes

Note that you want to buy a bit of extra asparagus so that you have the full ½ pound after you've trimmed it.

There are a ton of zesters on the market today. I like to use different ones for different applications. For this recipe, I like a thicker, almost thin ribbon type of zest. Given the coarseness of the asparagus, it works well. In a cake or muffin, I'd want a much finer zest. Want more specific advice from me on purchasing or using a zester? Have other questions regarding this book? I'm excited to help get (or keep) you on a path to eating that you enjoy and that honors your health. Visit me at **www.devinalexander.com/diabetes** and I'll do just that!

CHOICES/EXCHANGES
1 nonstarchy vegetable, ½ fat

PER SERVING
60 calories, 3.5 g fat, 0.5 g saturated fat, 0 g trans fat, 0 mg cholesterol, 150 mg sodium, 240 mg potassium, 6 g carbohydrate, 3 g fiber, 2 g sugars, 3 g protein, 60 mg phosphorus

Burst of Lemon Sautéed Spinach

Olive oil spray (propellant free)

1 tablespoon plus 1 teaspoon freshly minced garlic

½ cup chopped shallots

1 pound fresh baby spinach leaves or spinach leaves, coarse stems removed

2 tablespoons lemon zest

⅛ teaspoon sea salt

Freshly ground black pepper, to taste

Lemon wedges, for squeezing

1 Lightly mist a large nonstick frying pan with spray and place it over medium heat. Add the garlic and shallots and cook for approximately 3–5 minutes, until they are tender and just starting to brown.

2 Add the spinach leaves to the pan and place a lid that is smaller than the pan directly on top of the leaves (this weights them down). After a minute or two, the leaves will begin to expel water and start wilting. Remove the lid and, using tongs, stir the leaves until they are completely wilted and no water remains in pan.

3 Stir in the lemon zest and season with salt and pepper. Enjoy immediately with lemon wedges on the side for squeezing over the spinach, if desired.

Cook's Notes

Be sure not to zest any of the pith (the white part) of the lemon. The dish will become bitter if the pith is included.

CHOICES/EXCHANGES
2 nonstarchy vegetables

PER SERVING
50 calories, 1 g fat, 0 g saturated fat, 0 g trans fat, 0 mg cholesterol, 170 mg sodium, 715 mg potassium, 10 g carbohydrate, 3 g fiber, 1 g sugars, 4 g protein, 70 mg phosphorus

Hot Sesame Spinach

It always shocks me how much spinach shrinks when it's cooked. This recipe that calls for an entire pound of fresh spinach yields only a couple of cups. Make sure you take this into account when grocery shopping.

Olive oil spray (propellant free)

1 tablespoon plus 1 teaspoon freshly minced garlic

1 pound fresh spinach leaves, coarse stems removed (weighed after removing stems)

1 teaspoon hot pepper sesame oil

1 teaspoon toasted or roasted sesame oil

Freshly ground black pepper, to taste

¼ teaspoon toasted sesame seeds

1 Lightly mist a large nonstick frying pan with spray and place it over medium heat. Add the garlic and cook it for approximately 3–5 minutes, until it is tender and just starting to brown.

2 Add the spinach leaves to the pan. Place a lid that is smaller than the pan directly on top of the leaves (this weights them down). After a minute or two, the leaves will begin to expel water and start wilting. Remove the lid and, using tongs, stir the leaves intermittently until they are completely wilted and no water remains in pan.

3 Drizzle the hot pepper sesame oil and toasted sesame oil over top and season with the pepper.

4 Transfer the spinach to a serving bowl or divide it evenly among 4 dinner plates or bowls (about ½ cup in each). Top the spinach evenly with the sesame seeds. Enjoy immediately.

Cook's Notes

When buying hot pepper sesame oil, buy one that is toasted sesame oil infused with chilies. Not sesame oil and chilies. They taste very different.

CHOICES/EXCHANGES
1 nonstarchy vegetable, ½ fat

PER SERVING
50 calories, 3 g fat, 0.4 g saturated fat, 0 g trans fat, 0 mg cholesterol, 90 mg sodium, 650 mg potassium, 5 g carbohydrate, 3 g fiber, 1 g sugars, 3 g protein, 60 mg phosphorus

Green Beans with Champagne Vinaigrette

I keep Champagne Vinaigrette (see the recipe on page 186) in my refrigerator at all times—it's so great to have on hand when guests stop by last minute. It makes me look like such a chef to be able to whip up a gorgeous, special salad or side in seconds. Hint: you can look like a chef just as easily!

1 pound fresh green beans, ends trimmed

2 tablespoons plus ½ tablespoon Champagne Vinaigrette (see page 186), divided

1 tablespoon freshly minced shallots

1 teaspoon freshly minced garlic

2 teaspoons finely chopped fresh flat leaf parsley

⅛ teaspoon sea salt

Freshly ground black pepper, to taste, if desired

Steamer insert/rack

*If you have the Champagne Vinaigrette prepared.

1 Place a steamer insert in a large soup pot. Fill the pot with water so it reaches just below the steamer rack. Place the pot over high heat and bring the water to a boil. Add the green beans and cover the pot. Cook them until crisp tender, about 3–5 minutes.

2 Meanwhile, mix the vinaigrette, shallots, garlic, parsley, and salt in a small bowl.

3 Remove the green beans to a large glass or plastic bowl, making sure to drain any excess moisture from the beans. Gently toss the green beans with 2 tablespoons of the vinaigrette mixture. Season with pepper. Add the additional ½ tablespoon of vinaigrette mixture, if desired. Transfer the beans to a serving platter or divide among 4 plates. Enjoy immediately.

Cook's Notes

You only need to trim the tough end of green beans before steaming them. The other end is already smooth.

CHOICES/EXCHANGES
2 nonstarchy vegetables

PER SERVING
50 calories, 2 g fat, 0 g saturated fat, 0 g trans fat, 0 mg cholesterol, 105 mg sodium, 290 mg potassium, 8 g carbohydrate, 4 g fiber, 3 g sugars, 2 g protein, 0 mg phosphorus

Dijon Roasted Brussels Sprouts

I hated veggies as a kid. My mother can attest that I spit out the pea baby food she tried to feed me as a tiny baby. Now I eat plenty of veggies, but I still don't love most cooked vegetables. Brussels sprouts were one of my least favorites for the longest time, though in recent years I've been enjoying them a bit more thanks to recipes like this one. I hope you enjoy these too!

Don't know how to trim Brussels sprouts? No worries! I've got you covered. Come join me at www.devinalexander.com/diabetes and I'll show you how to do it—no fancy tools required!

1 pound Brussels sprouts

½ tablespoon extra virgin olive oil

2 teaspoons balsamic vinegar

2 teaspoons Dijon mustard

¼ teaspoon reduced sodium salt substitute

¼ teaspoon freshly ground black pepper, or to taste

Olive oil spray (propellant free)

1 Preheat the oven to 400°F. Line a medium baking sheet with nonstick foil.

2 Trim the ends of the Brussels sprouts and remove any tough or yellow outer leaves. Cut the sprouts in half.

3 In a small bowl, whisk together the olive oil, vinegar, and Dijon mustard until well combined. In a large glass or plastic bowl, toss the Brussels sprouts with the olive oil mixture until well coated. Season them with the salt substitute and pepper and toss them again.

4 Spread the sprouts on the prepared baking sheet in a single layer. Roast them for 10 minutes, then, using a rubber spatula, stir them on the pan (to make sure they brown evenly). Lightly mist them with spray. Continue baking until the sprouts are crisp tender and lightly browned in spots, about an additional 5–15 minutes (depending the size of the sprouts). Enjoy immediately.

CHOICES/EXCHANGES
2 nonstarchy vegetable, ½ fat

PER SERVING
70 calories, 3 g fat, 0.4 g saturated fat, 0 g trans fat, 0 mg cholesterol, 160 mg sodium, 450 mg potassium, 9 g carbohydrate, 3 g fiber, 2 g sugars, 3 g protein, 65 mg phosphorus

Sweet Papaya Slaw

I recommend buying preshredded green cabbage from the grocery store if you can find it. If not, make sure you shred it finely yourself. It makes for a much nicer slaw, especially given the other components in this recipe. Peak season for papayas is early summer and fall, so I try to make this slaw often during those times.

¼ cup plain fat free yogurt or quark

¼ cup light mayonnaise

⅓ cup 100% orange juice (not from concentrate; preferably freshly squeezed)

2 tablespoons white vinegar

1 teaspoon zero calorie natural sweetener

7 cups finely shredded green cabbage (about 10 ounces)

1 cup (¼ inch cubes) fresh, ripe papaya cubes

½ cup slivered red onion

¼ teaspoon sea salt

Freshly ground black pepper, to taste

1 In a large resealable plastic container, whisk together the yogurt, mayonnaise, orange juice, vinegar, and sweetener. Add the cabbage, papaya, and onion and stir until well combined.

2 Season with salt and pepper. Enjoy immediately or cover and refrigerate for up to 2 days.

CHOICES/EXCHANGES
½ fruit, 1 nonstarchy vegetable, ½ fat

PER SERVING
70 calories, 2.5 g fat, 0 g saturated fat, 0 g trans fat, 5 mg cholesterol, 210 mg sodium, 290 mg potassium, 14 g carbohydrate, 3 g fiber, 7 g sugars, 2 g protein, 35 mg phosphorus

Cucumber Jicama Carrot Slaw

*This recipe comes together extremely quickly if you have a mandolin that cuts matchsticks or a food processor attachment. Otherwise cutting can take a long time. Want to know what equipment I use? Visit me at **www.devinalexander.com/diabetes** and I'll show you!*

¼ cup freshly squeezed lime juice

½ tablespoon zero calorie natural sweetener

¼ teaspoon sea salt

2 teaspoons roasted or toasted sesame oil

1 cup carrot matchsticks

2 cups cucumber matchsticks

2 cups jicama matchsticks

1 In a small mixing bowl, using a whisk, stir the lime juice, sweetener, and salt together until the sweetener and salt dissolve. Slowly whisk in the sesame oil until well incorporated.

2 Add the carrots, cucumber, and jicama to a medium plastic or glass mixing bowl. Pour the dressing over top. Toss well. Refrigerate for 10 minutes.

3 Remove the slaw from the refrigerator. Toss the slaw again and divide it among 4 serving bowls or plates. Enjoy immediately or refrigerate it in a resealable container for up to 2 days.

CHOICES/EXCHANGES
2 nonstarchy vegetables, ½ fat

PER SERVING
70 calories, 2.5 g fat, 0 g saturated fat, 0 g trans fat, 0 mg cholesterol, 170 mg sodium, 270 mg potassium, 13 g carbohydrate, 4 g fiber, 4 g sugars, 1 g protein, 40 mg phosphorus

Simple Champagne Slaw

Champagne vinegar can add a flavor boost to so many dishes. This recipe is a great example. The ingredients are so simple, but the vinegar transforms it into an elegant side dish. I sometimes serve the slaw in a martini glass for fun. We eat with our eyes first, so why not strive for a beautiful presentation?

3 tablespoons champagne vinegar

1 tablespoon extra virgin olive oil

¼ teaspoon sea salt

¼ teaspoon reduced sodium salt substitute

½ teaspoon freshly minced garlic

2 tablespoons finely chopped fresh flat leaf parsley

6 cups shredded red cabbage (not packed)

1 In a small bowl, whisk together the vinegar and olive oil until well combined. Add the salt, salt substitute, garlic, and parsley and stir until well combined.

2 Add the cabbage to a large glass or plastic mixing bowl. Pour the dressing over the cabbage and toss until thoroughly mixed. Enjoy immediately.

CHOICES/EXCHANGES
1 nonstarchy vegetable, ½ fat

PER SERVING
45 calories, 2.5 g fat, 0.3 g saturated fat, 0 g trans fat, 0 mg cholesterol, 160 mg sodium, 230 mg potassium, 6 g carbohydrate, 1 g fiber, 3 g sugars, 1 g protein, 20 mg phosphorus

Spicy Sriracha Slaw

Slaw is one of my favorite "snacks". Even though I've kept off 70 pounds for several years, I'm still wired to love food and sometimes I want food at times when I'm not even hungry. High emotions, stress, and procrastination all trigger me to want to eat. So when I know I'm in "one of those moods," I make a big batch of slaw and keep it in my refrigerator for when the munchies strike!

3 tablespoons apple cider vinegar

½ tablespoon honey

1 tablespoon sriracha (preferably natural)

6 cups loosely packed, very finely shredded green cabbage

1 cup carrot matchsticks

¼ teaspoon reduced sodium salt substitute

⅛ teaspoon kosher salt

1 In a small bowl, whisk together the vinegar, honey, and sriracha until well combined.

2 Add the cabbage and carrots to a medium airtight container. Pour the sriracha mixture over the cabbage and carrots and toss until well combined.

3 Season with the salt substitute and salt. Cover the slaw and place it in the refrigerator for at least 20 minutes, or up to 2 days.

Cook's Notes

If you're enjoying this slaw as a component of a dish such as a taco, you'll likely agree it's perfectly seasoned with the amount of sriracha and salt called for in this recipe. But if you're eating it on its own, the average palate may find it a bit too spicy, and you may think that it could be enhanced with some extra salt. If you plan to eat the slaw by itself, start by adding ½ tablespoon sriracha and then add the additional to taste and add the salt to taste.

Instead of shredding the cabbage yourself, look for bagged angel hair cabbage in the produce section of your grocery store.

I suggest investing in a mandolin that allows you to cut matchsticks quickly. Don't know what I'm referencing? Visit me at **www.devinalexander.com/diabetes** and I will show you!

CHOICES/EXCHANGES
1 nonstarchy vegetable

PER SERVING
35 calories, 0 g fat, 0 g saturated fat, 0 g trans fat, 0 mg cholesterol, 180 mg sodium, 255 mg potassium, 7 g carbohydrate, 2 g fiber, 5 g sugars, 1 g protein, 25 mg phosphorus

Watermelon Street "Fries"

These "fries" are a twist on the fruit found in street fruit carts. They make a great snack; this recipe really transforms "plain" watermelon into a sweet and savory treat that's so nutritious. They're (obviously) incredibly easy to make and they're great for tossing in salads too!

4 ounces (about ¾ cup) seedless watermelon sticks (⅓ inch thick × 3 ½ inch long sticks)

1 teaspoon freshly squeezed lime juice

¹⁄₁₆ teaspoon chili powder

¹⁄₆₄ teaspoon sea salt

Pinch cayenne pepper

1 Place the watermelon sticks in a medium shallow bowl. Drizzle the lime juice over them, then sprinkle the chili powder, salt, and cayenne evenly over top. Gently toss them. Enjoy immediately.

CHOICES/EXCHANGES
½ fruit

PER SERVING
35 calories, 0 g fat, 0 g saturated fat, 0 g trans fat, 0 mg cholesterol, 40 mg sodium, 135 mg potassium, 9 g carbohydrate, 1 g fiber, 7 g sugars, 1 g protein, 15 mg phosphorus

CHAMPAGNE BLACKBERRY CHILLERS · 175

DEVINLY *Desserts* & SWEET *Sips*

Chocolate Peanut Butter Wafflewich Sliders

¼ cup high protein, low calorie, stevia sweetened chocolate ice cream (preferably natural)

4 mini whole grain waffles

2 teaspoons natural, smooth peanut butter (preferably just peanuts)

1 Remove the ice cream from the freezer to soften it slightly. When it's no longer super hard (you don't want it melting, but you don't want it too hard to manipulate into the sandwiches), toast the waffles until they are a light golden brown.

2 Spread the peanut butter over one side of two waffles (1 teaspoon per waffle). Place those two waffles on a plate, peanut butter side up. Add 2 tablespoons of the ice cream on top of each waffle with peanut butter (use an ice cream scoop 2 ½ inches in diameter for ease if you have one).

3 Lightly place one of the remaining waffles on top of each to make a sandwich. Then use a butter knife, as you push down the top of the sandwich, to nudge the ice cream into the sandwich. Repeat with the remaining sandwich. Enjoy immediately.

Cook's Notes

Not all whole grain waffles say that they are whole grain on the front of the package. Try to find waffles that are natural and contain as much fiber as possible.

CHOICES/EXCHANGES
½ starch, ½ carbohydrate, 1 high-fat protein

PER SERVING
180 calories, 9 g fat, 2.1 g saturated fat, 0 g trans fat, 20 mg cholesterol, 250 mg sodium, 190 mg potassium, 19 g carbohydrate, 3 g fiber, 4 g sugars, 7 g protein, 180 mg phosphorus

Truer Love in a Bowl

I developed a version of this recipe for a bodybuilder ex-boyfriend because he has a raging sweet tooth, but always wanted to make clean eating a priority. Ice cream was his go to comfort food. What better way to show my love for him than with super clean ingredients prepared with love? Friends have since fallen in love with this recipe. And it seems like everyone is making it since I published a version of it in The Biggest Loser Dessert Cookbook.

As someone who's lost 70 pounds and kept it off for many years, I actually consider this recipe "important" in my life. If you're like me, sometimes you just have to indulge in the perfect combo of chocolate and peanut butter! I always keep a few bananas in my freezer so I am ready when a chocolate and peanut butter craving hits. Just be sure to peel the bananas before you freeze them!

4 medium peeled frozen bananas (about 3 ½ ounces each)

3 tablespoons natural peanut butter

¼ cup unsweetened cocoa powder, or to taste

1 Break the bananas into a few pieces and place them in the bowl of a food processor fitted with a chopping blade. Add the peanut butter, then sprinkle the cocoa powder over the bananas.

2 Process the mixture on high, stopping the machine and scraping down the sides of the bowl as needed. It will take at least a few minutes for the bananas and cocoa powder to fully incorporate and become thick and creamy like ice cream. (Stick with it. The payoff is chocolate peanut butter decadence!)

3 Divide the mixture among 4 martini glasses, heart shaped ramekins, or other small bowls and enjoy immediately.

Cook's Notes

If you want the banana flavor to shine through, use just 2 tablespoons of cocoa powder. If you're like me and prefer this dessert to more closely resemble chocolate ice cream, use up to 4 tablespoons.

CHOICES/EXCHANGES
1 ½ fruit, ½ carbohydrate, 1 fat

PER SERVING
170 calories, 7 g fat, 1.3 g saturated fat, 0 g trans fat, 0 mg cholesterol, 45 mg sodium, 520 mg potassium, 28 g carbohydrate, 5 g fiber, 13 g sugars, 5 g protein, 105 mg phosphorus

Quick Berry Crumbles à la Mode

6 cups fresh mixed berries

1 ½ tablespoons plus ½ tablespoon zero calorie natural sweetener, divided

2 tablespoons plus 2 tablespoons whole grain oat flour, divided

30 grams (about ⅓ cup) stevia sweetened natural vanilla protein powder

½ teaspoon ground cinnamon

1 ½ tablespoons vegan butter (from a stick, not a tub)

1 ½ cups high protein, low calorie, stevia sweetened vanilla ice cream (preferably natural)

1 Preheat the oven to 400°F.

2 In a medium mixing bowl, stir together the berries, 1 ½ tablespoons of the sweetener, and 2 tablespoons of flour until well combined. Spoon the mixed berries evenly (about ¾ cup in each) among 6 ramekins (4 ½ inches in diameter; 1–1 ½ cups capacity). Place the ramekins on a baking sheet large enough to hold them in a single layer so they sit flat.

3 Add the remaining 2 tablespoons of flour, the protein powder, the remaining ½ tablespoon of sweetener, the cinnamon, and the vegan butter to a small mixing bowl. Using a fork or pastry blender, stir the flour mixture together to create a crumble. Divide the crumble evenly over the top of the fruit in the ramekins (about 1 ½ tablespoons per ramekin).

4 Bake until the crumble is golden on top and the berries are hot throughout, about 14–20 minutes. Let the crumbles cool for 3 minutes. Top each with ¼ cup of ice cream to enjoy immediately. Cover any remaining crumbles with plastic wrap and store them in the refrigerator for up to 3 days. Reheat them in the oven then top them with ice cream just before enjoying.

Cook's Notes

I've made these crumbles with many variations of berries—usually whichever are freshest, most plentiful, and, thus, often on sale. As a default, I'll use 2 cups of blueberries, 2 cups of strawberries, and 2 cups of raspberries. If using strawberries, they will need to be trimmed and chopped to be about the size of the blueberries and raspberries for best results.

Make sure to use gluten free oat flour if you're gluten intolerant or serving this dessert to guests who are.

Make sure you use a protein powder that doesn't have an aftertaste.

CHOICES/EXCHANGES
1 fruit, ½ carbohydrate, 1 lean protein, ½ fat

PER SERVING
150 calories, 4.5 g fat, 1.3 g saturated fat, 0 g trans fat, 20 mg cholesterol, 85 mg sodium, 290 mg potassium, 25 g carbohydrate, 7 g fiber, 12 g sugars, 8 g protein, 110 mg phosphorus

QUICK BERRY CRUMBLES À LA MODE

Dark Chocolate "Pudding"

½ cup fat free vanilla quark

½ tablespoon zero calorie natural sweetener

3 tablespoons special dark 100% cocoa powder

1/32 teaspoon sea salt

1 tablespoon Devinly Whipped Topping (see page 178)

*If you have the Devinly Whipped Topping prepared.

1 In a small mixing bowl or storage container, mix the quark, sweetener, and cocoa powder until there are no lumps at all and the ingredients are well combined.

2 Transfer the mixture to a martini glass or serving bowl (or prepare to just dig in!). Sprinkle the salt over top. Add the whipped topping. Enjoy immediately.

Cook's Notes

Though quark seems like yogurt, it's actually a cheese. I've become a huge fan of quark in recent years because it's even better for you than Greek yogurt. A half cup of my favorite brand of fat free vanilla quark (which is natural even though it doesn't have fat) has only 4.5 g of sugar, while ½ cup of vanilla Greek yogurt tends to have about 12.5 g of sugar.

Want to try quark and interested in which brand I use? Pop over to **www.devinalexander.com/diabetes** and I'll share that along with plenty of chef secrets and so much more.

CHOICES/EXCHANGES
1 carbohydrate, 1 lean protein

PER SERVING
100 calories, 2.5 g fat, 1.4 g saturated fat, 0 g trans fat, 0 mg cholesterol, 105 mg sodium, 410 mg potassium, 19 g carbohydrate, 5 g fiber, 6 g sugars, 13 g protein, 275 mg phosphorus

SERVES: 2 • SERVING SIZE: ½ of the pears + ¼ cup ice cream • PREP TIME: 15 minutes • COOK TIME: 30–40 minutes

Pear "Fries" à la Mode

Have you ever tried baked pears? I like them more when baked than raw. I can't believe how easily this fruit can be transformed without requiring much extra effort. The sweetness really comes out! (And I have a huge sweet tooth!)

Not sure about any of the ingredients listed below? I've set up plenty of resources for you at www.devinalexander.com/diabetes. I want to make this so easy for you! It's time for everyone to eat decadently while enjoying good health!

Canola oil spray (propellant free)

2 medium (about 6–8 ounce) pears

2 teaspoons freshly squeezed lime juice

½ tablespoon zero calorie natural sweetener

2 teaspoons melted vegan butter (from a stick, not a tub)

⅛ teaspoon cinnamon

½ cup high protein, low calorie, stevia sweetened vanilla ice cream (preferably natural)

1 Preheat the oven to 300°F. Line a medium baking sheet with nonstick foil. Lightly mist it with spray.

2 Peel the pears. Cut ½ inch thick sticks from the pears, avoiding the cores (cut off the sides as close to the cores as possible, then cut the sides into sticks), until you have 8 ounces of sticks (about 1 ¼ cups).

3 Transfer the pear sticks to a small mixing bowl. Add the lime juice, sweetener, butter, and cinnamon. Using a rubber spatula, gently mix them until the sticks are evenly coated.

4 Place the sticks on the prepared baking sheet and bake them for 15 minutes. Flip them, and continue baking them until they are golden brown and soft throughout, about 15–25 minutes, flipping them one more time if they are getting browned on one side more than the other. Divide the "fries" among 2 shallow dessert bowls. Top each with ¼ cup of ice cream. Enjoy immediately.

CHOICES/EXCHANGES
1 fruit, ½ carbohydrate, 1 fat

PER SERVING
130 calories, 5 g fat, 1.5 g saturated fat, 0 g trans fat, 20 mg cholesterol, 90 mg sodium, 200 mg potassium, 24 g carbohydrate, 5 g fiber, 14 g sugars, 3 g protein, 50 mg phosphorus

Apple "Fries" with Creamy Peanut Butter Dip

Apples and peanut butter are obviously a great snack, but they can also be a little humdrum. My Creamy Peanut Butter Dip (see page 179) turns this dish into a bit more of an indulgence. I do truly love this dessert, as will you and your kids! It's even a great dip for a child's birthday party.

2 extra large apples (about 10 ounces each)

1 tablespoon freshly squeezed lemon juice

12 tablespoons Creamy Peanut Butter Dip (see page 179)

*If you have the Creamy Peanut Butter Dip prepared.

1 Avoiding the core, cut the apples into sticks that are about ⅓ inch thick and as long as the height of the apple so they look similar to French fries.

2 Transfer the "fries" to a medium glass or plastic serving bowl and toss them with the lemon juice until they are evenly coated.

3 Divide the dip among 4 small dipping containers or bowls (about 3 tablespoons in each). Enjoy immediate with the fries.

CHOICES/EXCHANGES
1 fruit, 1 high-fat protein

PER SERVING
150 calories, 6 g fat, 0.8 g saturated fat, 0 g trans fat, 0 mg cholesterol, 60 mg sodium, 240 mg potassium, 18 g carbohydrate, 3 g fiber, 13 g sugars, 7 g protein, 100 mg phosphorus

Lemon Blueberry Ricotta Tartlets

Make sure to finely grate lemon zest for this recipe! Not sure exactly what that means? No worries! Come see me at www.devinalexander.com/diabetes and I'll show you! Plus I'll share chef secrets, fill you in on my favorite brands, and so much more!

¾ cup fat free ricotta cheese

3 large egg whites (preferably cage free)

1 tablespoon zero calorie natural sweetener

¾ teaspoon vanilla extract

1 tablespoon freshly grated lemon zest

24 mini fillo cups

24 fresh blueberries

1 Preheat the oven to 350°F. Line a small baking sheet with nonstick foil.

2 In a small mixing bowl, using a spoon, mix the ricotta, egg whites, sweetener, vanilla, and lemon zest until well combined. Divide the mixture evenly among the fillo cups (about 1 tablespoon per cup). Then use the back of the spoon to level the tops.

3 Place the filled cups side by side on the lined baking sheet. Bake them until the filling is warm and the shells are a light golden brown, about 14–18 minutes.

4 Allow them to cool for 3 minutes. Divide the blueberries evenly among them, placing them on top of the filling. Enjoy immediately.

Cook's Notes

Mini fillo cups can be found in the freezer section of your grocery store. If you're not serving them all at once, make the filling and fill the cups you plan to serve or eat. Refrigerate the remaining filling in an airtight container (for up to 3 days); fill and bake the fillo cups just before serving.

CHOICES/EXCHANGES
1 carbohydrate

PER SERVING
80 calories, 1.5 g fat, 0 g saturated fat, 0 g trans fat, 0 mg cholesterol, 80 mg sodium, 25 mg potassium, 11 g carbohydrate, 0 g fiber, 3 g sugars, 5 g protein, 0 mg phosphorus

WATERMELON "CUPCAKES"

Watermelon "Cupcakes"

1 medium to large seedless watermelon (you'll have plenty left over)

8 tablespoons Devinly Whipped Topping (see page 178)

8 blueberries

⅛ teaspoon edible red glitter (made from gelatin, not sugar)

1 cupcake shaped cookie cutter (about 3 inches tall with a base about 2 ½ inches wide)

*If you have the Devinly Whipped Topping prepared.

1 Trim away one end of the watermelon. Cut a slice that's about ½ inch thick from the melon. Making sure not to include any of the white portion of the watermelon, use the cookie cutter to cut as many "cupcakes" from the slice as you can (you should get about 2–3 per slice, depending on the size of your watermelon). Continue cutting slices and using the cookie cutter to cut cupcakes until you have 8 cupcakes.

2 Place the cupcakes on a clean work surface. Using a pastry bag with a relatively small hole (I used a #10 tip, which pretty accurately yielded 1 tablespoon of topping, but you can use any tip), frost the top portion of the cupcakes with the whipped topping. Sprinkle the glitter evenly over the frosted portions. Place a blueberry on the top of each. Enjoy immediately.

Cook's Notes

Never used a pastry bag? I'll show you how! Go to www.devinalexander.com/diabetes for a lesson in cupcake decorating, and the specifics on the glitter and cookie cutter I use for these scrumptious cupcakes!

Be sure that the glitter you use is made from gelatin instead of sugar! You probably won't even need the full ⅛ teaspoon of glitter—a little goes a long way.

To make sure you're using the correct amount of frosting, you can frost one then scrape the whipped topping into a 1 tablespoon measuring spoon, which will give you a sense of how much you are actually using. If it's less than 1 tablespoon, put more pressure on the tip when you frost the cupcake, or if it's more, put less pressure.

If you can't find a cookie cutter that is exactly the same size as mine, don't worry! Just make sure the one you use is 1 inch deep and metal; this will make it much easier to cut the watermelon than it would be with a plastic one. A serving is basically 2 ½ ounces of watermelon with 1 tablespoon of whipped topping and 1 blueberry, which contains 30 calories and 6 g of sugars. As long as you stick to those serving guidelines, you can create "cupcakes" of any shape or size that are just as festive!

CHOICES/EXCHANGES
½ carbohydrate

PER SERVING
30 calories, 0 g fat, 0 g saturated fat, 0 g trans fat, 0 mg cholesterol, 0 mg sodium, 85 mg potassium, 7 g carbohydrate, 0 g fiber, 6 g sugars, 1 g protein, 10 mg phosphorus

Grilled Peaches with Amaretto Ricotta & Toasted Almonds

I often find that a tiny amount of alcohol can really elevate a dish. Here, a simple ½ tablespoon of amaretto liqueur works like a charm to turn these peaches into a satisfying adult dessert.

⅓ cup low fat ricotta cheese

½ teaspoon zero calorie natural sweetener

½ tablespoon amaretto liqueur

1 slightly firm medium peach (about 5 ounces), cut in half and stone removed

Canola oil spray (propellant free)

1 tablespoon toasted chopped almonds

1 Preheat a grill to medium heat.

2 In a small bowl, combine the ricotta, sweetener, and amaretto. Mix until well combined.

3 Lightly mist the cut sides of the peach halves with spray. Place them, cut sides down, on the grill (place away from direct flame if the grill can't be set to medium heat). Grill them until they have grill marks and are warmed through, about 3 minutes.

4 Place the peach halves on a serving plate. Divide the ricotta mixture evenly between them, spooning it over the center of the peaches. Sprinkle the toasted almonds on top. Enjoy immediately.

CHOICES/EXCHANGES
1 fruit, ½ carbohydrate, 1 lean protein, 1 fat

PER SERVING
200 calories, 7 g fat, 2.3 g saturated fat, 0 g trans fat, 20 mg cholesterol, 120 mg sodium, 430 mg potassium, 24 g carbohydrate, 3 g fiber, 21 g sugars, 11 g protein, 210 mg phosphorus

Grilled Pear Boats with Romano, Walnuts & Black Pepper

I don't think it's a secret that in many European countries people enjoy fruit and cheese instead of the sweet desserts that we often end meals with here in the U.S. These grilled pears with Romano are an ode, of sorts, to my Italian ancestry. While I honestly could never completely trade in my chocolate for this dish, I do find it to be a very unique, welcome change from time to time. I hope you will give it a try and enjoy it as much as I do!

1 pear (about 6–7 ounces), halved and core scraped out

Canola oil spray (propellant free)

½ ounce coarsely shredded Pecorino Romano cheese (preferably natural)

1 tablespoon finely chopped Can-Have Candied Pecans (see page 180)

Freshly ground black pepper, to taste

*If you have the Can-Have Candied Pecans prepared.

1 Preheat the grill to high.

2 Cut a small slice from the rounded (skin) side of each pear half so when the pear boat is core side up, it sits flat. Cut the stem from the pear, leaving the pear otherwise intact. Place the pear halves core side up on a cutting board. Lightly mist them with spray.

3 Turn the grill to low (or make sure you place the pears away from direct flame if you can't turn the grill to low). Place the pear halves side by side, core side down, on the grill. Grill them until the pears are warmed through and have grill marks, approximately 3 minutes. Carefully flip them and (being careful not to burn yourself) sprinkle the cheese evenly over the tops. Continue grilling them just until the cheese melts, about 1 minute.

4 Transfer each half to a separate serving plate. Sprinkle the pecans evenly over top. Season with pepper. Enjoy immediately.

CHOICES/EXCHANGES
1 fruit, 1 fat

PER SERVING
110 calories, 5 g fat, 1.6 g saturated fat, 0 g trans fat, 5 mg cholesterol, 90 mg sodium, 125 mg potassium, 14 g carbohydrate, 3 g fiber, 9 g sugars, 3 g protein, 75 mg phosphorus

Perfect Pumpkin Pie-lets

9 mini fillo shells

2 large egg whites (preferably cage free)

¼ cup solid pumpkin purée

1 teaspoon maple syrup

1 teaspoon zero calorie natural sweetener

1 teaspoon brown sugar

½ tablespoon whole grain oat flour

½ teaspoon vanilla extract

¼ teaspoon plus ⅛ teaspoon pumpkin pie spice

¼ teaspoon ground cinnamon

⅛ teaspoon baking powder

1/16 teaspoon salt

9 teaspoons Devinly Whipped Topping (see page 178)

*If you have the Devinly Whipped Topping prepared.

1 Preheat the oven to 350°F. Line a small baking sheet with nonstick foil. Place the fillo shells side by side on the baking sheet so they don't touch.

2 In a small mixing bowl, using a sturdy whisk, mix the egg whites, pumpkin, maple syrup, sweetener, brown sugar, and flour together until well combined. Still using the whisk, stir in the vanilla, pumpkin pie spice, cinnamon, baking powder, and salt and continue mixing until well combined. Divide the filling among the fillo shells, about 1 tablespoon in each.

3 Bake the pie-lets for 10–15 minutes, or until a toothpick inserted into the center comes out sticky (it shouldn't be runny, but won't be dry). Allow them to cool to room temperature. Just before serving, top each pie-let with 1 teaspoon whipped topping. Enjoy immediately.

Cook's Notes

If you want just one serving of these pie-lets, fill and bake that serving, then store the rest of the filling in the refrigerator. Fill the remaining shells and bake them just before you plan to enjoy them, otherwise the shells will become soggy.

CHOICES/EXCHANGES
1 carbohydrate, ½ fat

PER SERVING
100 calories, 3 g fat, 0.1 g saturated fat, 0 g trans fat, 0 mg cholesterol, 140 mg sodium, 105 mg potassium, 13 g carbohydrate, 1 g fiber, 5 g sugars, 3 g protein, 45 mg phosphorus

PERFECT PUMPKIN PIE-LETS

Strawberry Daiquiri Sorbet

This is a great summer treat. The rum can elevate what might otherwise be a generic dessert. And the best part? It's so simple to make!

4 cups frozen strawberries

3 tablespoons dark rum

2 tablespoons freshly squeezed lime juice

½ tablespoon stevia honey blend sweetener (such as Truvia Nectar)

1 tablespoon zero calorie natural sweetener

1 Place the strawberries, rum, lime juice, honey blend sweetener, and zero calorie natural sweetener in a food processor fitted with a chopping blade.

2 Process the mixture on high, using a spatula to scrape down the inside of the bowl as needed, until the strawberries are finely chopped and the ingredients are well incorporated. Enjoy immediately.

CHOICES/EXCHANGES
1 fruit

PER SERVING
90 calories, 0 g fat, 0 g saturated fat, 0 g trans fat, 0 mg cholesterol, 0 mg sodium, 230 mg potassium, 20 g carbohydrate, 3 g fiber, 10 g sugars, 0 g protein, 20 mg phosphorus

In-The-Clear Root Beer Float

*If you're a fan of diet soda, you've hopefully "switched over" to a naturally sweetened version. I was excited to create a modern day root beer float sweetened with stevia. I found a number of brands of zero calorie, stevia sweetened root beer, and I use my favorite high protein, stevia sweetened ice cream (the entire pint is only 240 calories!) for this recipe. If you don't have a favorite stevia sweetened soda or high protein ice cream and you want to learn what I'm using, visit **www.devinalexander.com/diabetes** where I share many of my favorite brands, cooking equipment, and even chef secrets!*

1 cup stevia sweetened, zero calorie root beer, chilled

½ cup high protein, low calorie, stevia sweetened vanilla ice cream (preferably natural)

1 Place a 12 ounce glass on a plate. Pour the root beer into the glass. Spoon the ice cream into the glass. Allow the ice cream to melt slightly, about 3–5 minutes. Enjoy immediately!

CHOICES/EXCHANGES
½ fat-free milk, ½ carbohydrate

PER SERVING
60 calories, 2 g fat, 1 g saturated fat, 0 g trans fat, 40 mg cholesterol, 115 mg sodium, 130 mg potassium, 13 g carbohydrate, 3 g fiber, 5 g sugars, 5 g protein, 65 mg phosphorus

Passionila Cocktail

1 passion tea bag (no sugar or caffeine)

6 ounces piping hot water

1–1 ½ teaspoons zero calorie natural sweetener

2 tablespoons lime liqueur (lime infused tequila)

1 ½ tablespoons freshly squeezed lime juice

6 ice cubes

1 lime slice, for garnish

1 Add the tea bag and water to a glass measuring cup that holds at least 1 cup. Brew the tea for 10 minutes. When cool enough to handle, squeeze the tea bag over the tea to capture optimum potency, and then discard the bag.

2 Pour the tea into a cocktail shaker. Add the sweetener, liqueur, lime juice, and ice cubes. Shake until chilled. Strain into a 10 ounce highball glass or an 8 ounce martini glass. Garnish with the lime slice. Serve immediately.

CHOICES/EXCHANGES
1 carbohydrate, ½ alcohol

PER SERVING
110 calories, 0 g fat, 0 g saturated fat, 0 g trans fat, 0 mg cholesterol, 15 mg sodium, 115 mg potassium, 13 g carbohydrate, 0 g fiber, 11 g sugars, 0 g protein, 5 mg phosphorus

PASSIONILA COCKTAIL

Sexy Trainer's Strawberry Caipirinha

If you are not familiar, a caipirinha is a Brazilian cocktail. I served this refreshing cocktail at my restaurants on Royal Caribbean Cruise line and passengers raved! This caipirinha is best served when strawberries are in the peak season—during the summer months. Make sure you muddle them until they're really pulverized...you don't want to have to chew your cocktail.

⅔ cup sliced fresh strawberries

1 tablespoon freshly squeezed lime juice

1 teaspoon zero calorie natural sweetener

1 ounce cachaça (a Brazilian liqueur)

½ cup crushed ice

1 whole strawberry, for garnish

1 Place the strawberries and lime juice into an old fashioned glass and muddle them until the strawberries are very finely mashed.

2 Transfer the strawberry mixture to a shaker. Add the sweetener, cachaça, and ice. Shake about 20 times until all of the ingredients are well combined and chilled. Pour back into the old fashioned glass. Enjoy immediately with the strawberry for garnish.

Cook's Notes

Cachaça, an essential ingredient in a caipirinha, is a Brazilian liqueur that can be found in most major liquor stores.

CHOICES/EXCHANGES
1 fruit, ½ alcohol

PER SERVING
110 calories, 0 g fat, 0 g saturated fat, 0 g trans fat, 0 mg cholesterol, 0 mg sodium, 200 mg potassium, 14 g carbohydrate, 2 g fiber, 6 g sugars, 1 g protein, 30 mg phosphorus

Champagne Blackberry Chillers

I love this cocktail around the holidays! It makes me feel festive and allows me to participate in the party without overconsuming alcohol. The berries will keep the champagne chilled, so you won't need to drink it quickly. Plus, they'll turn the champagne a red color to keep with the spirit of the season! Cheers!

16 frozen blackberries

1 cup chilled champagne

2 cocktail sticks

1 Divide the frozen blackberries between 2 champagne flutes (¾ cup capacity). Pour the champagne over the blackberries, ½ cup in each flute.

2 Add a festive cocktail stick (to use later for spearing any berries that remain in the bottom of the glass). Serve immediately.

CHOICES/EXCHANGES

½ fruit, 1 alcohol

PER SERVING

130 calories, 0 g fat, 0 g saturated fat, 0 g trans fat, 0 mg cholesterol, 5 mg sodium, 200 mg potassium, 10 g carbohydrate, 4 g fiber, 5 g sugars, 1 g protein, 35 mg phosphorus

DARK CHOCOLATE "PUDDING" • 160 | DEVINLY WHIPPED TOPPING • 178

Dressings, Sauces, Dips & Toppings

Devinly Whipped Topping

I love this whipped topping! I originally made a version for the Biggest Loser Dessert Cookbook *that I was very proud of at the time, and I even served it at Devinly Decadence, my restaurants on Royal Caribbean Cruise line. But I found that I was eating it too quickly because it wasn't holding up very long. So I went back to the kitchen and figured out how to stabilize it! This version will hold in the freezer for up to 2 weeks! (It never stays around that long in my house, but it could!) And if you serve it at a party on a dessert table, it won't flop on you in minutes.*

3 large egg whites (preferably cage free), at room temperature

½ teaspoon cream of tartar

¼ teaspoon xanthan gum

¾ cup light agave nectar

Cook's Notes

Note that this recipe could yield as many as 8 cups. With a recipe like this, there are so many factors that play into how aerated the topping becomes. If it yields more than 6 cups for you, then it will have even fewer calories and fewer grams of sugar than listed. I've never seen this recipe yield less than 6 cups, so, to be safe, we based the nutrition information on that yield for anyone who needs to closely monitor their nutritional intake.

Look for xanthan gum in the baking section or the natural foods aisle of major grocery stores or natural foods stores. I know this ingredient sounds scary, but I promise it's not a chemical!

1 Add the egg whites, cream of tartar, and xanthan gum to the bowl of a stand mixer and mix on medium speed until combined and the egg whites have just started to foam.

2 Pour the agave into a small saucepan and place it over medium heat. Making sure to watch it very carefully, heat the agave until it comes to a boil (it boils quickly and may burn if unattended even for a few seconds).

3 Turn the mixer to high and slowly and carefully pour the hot agave into the mixer (stand back, making sure that it does not accidentally splatter on you). Let it continue to whip until the topping is very thick and fluffy, has very stiff peaks, and has turned white.

4 Enjoy immediately and transfer any leftovers to an airtight plastic container and store in the freezer for up to 2 weeks.

CHOICES/EXCHANGES

This recipe has less than 20 calories and 5 g or less of carbohydrate per serving.

PER SERVING

10 calories, 0 g fat, 0 g saturated fat, 0 g trans fat, 0 mg cholesterol, 0 mg sodium, 0 mg potassium, 2 g carbohydrate, 0 g fiber, 2 g sugars, 0 g protein, 0 mg phosphorus

Creamy Peanut Butter Dip

This peanut butter dip is so delicious it's a bit dangerous...I could seriously overeat it. I am the biggest peanut butter lover. I definitely have to exert willpower (which I have very little of!) to resist anything peanut butter or chocolate. If you're anything like me, I'm sure you'll love it too.

½ cup plus 1 tablespoon plain fat free quark or fat free Greek yogurt

3 tablespoons natural, smooth peanut butter

1 tablespoon zero calorie natural sweetener

1 Add the quark, peanut butter, and sweetener to a small mixing bowl or resealable plastic container. Using a mini whisk or a spoon, mix the ingredients until well combined. Enjoy immediately.

Cook's Notes

Choose a natural peanut butter with only peanuts and salt in the ingredient list.

CHOICES/EXCHANGES
1 high-fat protein

PER SERVING
90 calories, 6 g fat, 0.8 g saturated fat, 0 g trans fat, 0 mg cholesterol, 55 mg sodium, 125 mg potassium, 4 g carbohydrate, 1 g fiber, 2 g sugars, 6 g protein, 85 mg phosphorus

Can-Have Candied Pecans

1 teaspoon melted vegan butter
(from a stick, not a tub)

1 teaspoon stevia cane sugar blend
(such as Truvia Cane Sugar Blend)

1/16 teaspoon pure vanilla extract

1/4 cup chopped pecans

1 Mix the butter, stevia blend, and vanilla in a small bowl.

2 Place a small nonstick frying pan over medium heat. Add the pecans. Toast them, stirring occasionally, until aromatic and dark brown in color, about 3–5 minutes. Turn off the heat and stir in butter mixture. Make sure the pecans are evenly coated.

3 Transfer the pecans to parchment paper in a single layer to cool.

CHOICES/EXCHANGES
1 fat

PER SERVING
60 calories, 6 g fat, 0.7 g saturated fat, 0 g trans fat, 0 mg cholesterol, 10 mg sodium, 30 mg potassium, 1 g carbohydrate, 1 g fiber, 1 g sugars, 1 g protein, 20 mg phosphorus

Garlicky Dill Dip & Sauce

I love this dip so much! After I developed this recipe, I became slightly addicted to it. That being said, the garlic gets stronger as the flavors meld, so after it's refrigerated for more than a few hours it does have a strong garlic taste (I stop eating it a couple days before date night just to be safe). If you aren't making this dip for a party, you might want to pull back on the garlic just a bit. Then you can continue to eat it all day if you'd like!

2 cups plain fat free Greek yogurt

2 tablespoons plus 2 teaspoons extra virgin olive oil

¼ cup finely chopped fresh dill leaves

1 ½ tablespoons freshly minced garlic

¾ teaspoon sea salt

1 In a small mixing bowl, mix the yogurt, olive oil, dill, garlic, and salt. Transfer the mixture to a resealable plastic container and chill for at least 2 hours (this dip can be made up to 2 days ahead; Keep refrigerated).

Cook's Notes

If I could bestow one tip upon you, it might actually be to always mince your garlic from actual cloves just before you are ready to use it (unless you're purposefully mashing it to mix with salt or using some other fancy culinary technique). But when a recipe calls for minced garlic, I can't possibly emphasize the importance of forgoing the use of preminced, jarred garlic. These products are often covered in oil, which contributes unnecessary calories, or mixed with citric acid, which will just plain ruin your dish!

CHOICES/EXCHANGES

½ fat

PER SERVING

30 calories, 2 g fat, 0.3 g saturated fat, 0 g trans fat, 0 mg cholesterol, 90 mg sodium, 35 mg potassium, 1 g carbohydrate, 0 g fiber, 1 g sugars, 2 g protein, 30 mg phosphorus

Skinny Dip in a Flash

Two tablespoons of a typical creamy dip have about 110 calories, 10 g of fat and 3 g of saturated fat. My Skinny Dip in a Flash has only 35 calories for about ¼ cup—so it's about 17 calories (rather than 110 calories) for 2 tablespoons with no saturated fat. This dip also doubles as a great spread for tacos and burritos.

1 (6 ounce) container (about ⅔ cup) plain fat free quark or fat free Greek yogurt

2 teaspoons salt free Mexican seasoning

⅛ teaspoon salt

1 Add the quark or yogurt, seasoning, and salt to a small resealable glass or plastic container. Using a fork or mini whisk, mix the ingredients until well combined. Refrigerate the dip for at least 30 minutes, or up to 3 days, before enjoying.

CHOICES/EXCHANGES
1 lean protein

PER SERVING
35 calories, 0 g fat, 0.1 g saturated fat, 0 g trans fat, 0 mg cholesterol, 115 mg sodium, 100 mg potassium, 3 g carbohydrate, 0 g fiber, 2 g sugars, 6 g protein, 80 mg phosphorus

Creamy Carrot Top Pesto

This pesto is almost more of a dip than a traditional pesto. I love it with roasted carrots (see page 142), but it's also an excellent sandwich spread, a unique dip for your party veggie platter, and so much more!

2 cups (about 1 ounce) loosely packed fresh carrot tops (leaves plucked from stems), roughly chopped

1 cup (about ¾ ounce) loosely packed fresh basil leaves

1 teaspoon freshly minced garlic

¾ cup plain fat free Greek yogurt

1 tablespoon grated Parmesan cheese (preferably natural)

1 tablespoon freshly squeezed lemon juice

2 tablespoons extra virgin olive oil

¼ teaspoon kosher salt

⅛ teaspoon reduced sodium salt substitute

1 Place the carrot tops, basil, garlic, yogurt, Parmesan, lemon juice, olive oil, salt, and salt substitute in a food processor fitted with a chopping blade. Process the ingredients until they are smooth. Enjoy immediately or store in an airtight container for up to 3 days.

Cook's Notes

It's important that you always wash your herbs—and that you dry them well! For optimal results, you want to follow recipes as written, and if you try to chop wet herbs, your yields could be way off. Wet basil leaves, for instance, will be much denser in a measuring cup than dry basil leaves. When making this creamy pesto, extra moisture will make it watery.

I strongly recommend that you wash and dry all of your herbs as soon as they arrive in your house. That will make it easier to grab basil leaves to flavor that salad or some cilantro to zip up those tacos without washing and drying them every time you want to use them. If you store fresh herbs in bags with a dry paper towel loosely covering them, the paper towel will pull away any excess moisture that builds over time... and they'll last much longer. For more on how to store herbs and so much more, visit **www.devinalexander.com/diabetes**.

CHOICES/EXCHANGES

1 fat

PER SERVING

50 calories, 4 g fat, 0.7 g saturated fat, 0 g trans fat, 0 mg cholesterol, 105 mg sodium, 85 mg potassium, 1 g carbohydrate, 0 g fiber, 1 g sugars, 3 g protein, 40 mg phosphorus

Renovated Ranch

I love sharing my recipes and creating dishes that I think people will enjoy! The biggest frustration for me is that different brands of the same food vary so widely, that my healthy creations could be "destroyed" depending on what brand is used. When I finally perfected this recipe, I was blown away by how closely it resembled full fat ranch dressing. But when my final recipe tester made it, it didn't taste nearly as good. We realized that she used a different light mayo (a vegan one) than I did. So I've set up a section on my website so you can learn what brands of ingredients I'm actually using at any given time. Feel free to substitute for different brands anytime you like, but if you want to make the recipes the way they were intended, pop over to www.devinalexander.com/diabetes for the inside scoop on brands and secret chef tips and tricks!

¼ cup light mayonnaise

¼ cup plain fat free Greek yogurt

½ cup low fat buttermilk

1 tablespoon finely chopped fresh flat leaf parsley

1 teaspoon dried dill

1 teaspoon dried minced onion

½ teaspoon dried garlic flakes, chopped or dried minced garlic

½ teaspoon dry mustard

¼ teaspoon freshly ground black pepper

⅛ teaspoon reduced sodium salt substitute

1 In a small mixing bowl, using a small whisk, mix the mayonnaise, yogurt, buttermilk, parsley, dill, onion, garlic, dry mustard, pepper, and salt substitute. Transfer the mixture to an airtight container and refrigerate it for at least 1 hour, or up to 2 days.

CHOICES/EXCHANGES
½ fat

PER SERVING
35 calories, 2 g fat, 0.3 g saturated fat, 0 g trans fat, 2 mg cholesterol, 95 mg sodium, 70 mg potassium, 2 g carbohydrate, 0 g fiber, 2 g sugars, 1 g protein, 30 mg phosphorus

Rockin' Body Balsamic

When purchasing balsamic vinegar, do a quick scan of the nutrition labels to make sure you're buying one with as little sugar and as few calories as possible. I know a lot of people think that vinegars have zero calories, but that's not at all true of balsamic vinegars.

I love making this simple dressing in the single serve cup of my blender. Then I store it in a salad cruet so I have it on hand at all times. That way I never need to worry about having added sugars or salt in my dressing!

½ **cup balsamic vinegar**

¼ **cup Dijon mustard**

¼ **cup extra virgin olive oil**

1 Add the vinegar and mustard to a small mixing bowl. Using a small whisk, slowly whisk in the oil until it is emulsified (well combined). Use immediately or refrigerate in an airtight container or salad cruet for up to 2 months.

CHOICES/EXCHANGES

1 fat

PER SERVING

40 calories, 3.5 g fat, 0.5 g saturated fat, 0 g trans fat, 0 mg cholesterol, 90 mg sodium, 15 mg potassium, 2 g carbohydrate, 0 g fiber, 1 g sugars, 0 g protein, 0 mg phosphorus

Champagne Vinaigrette

I love making this dressing in the single serve cup of my blender. Then I store it in a salad cruet so I have it on hand at all times and never need to worry about having tons of added sugars or sodium in my dressing!

Champagne vinegar is so under used in my opinion. So many people use white vinegar, apple cider vinegar, balsamic vinegar, and even rice vinegar. In addition to those, my pantry is stocked with champagne vinegar, port vinegar, and even cabernet vinegar. Sure, the latter vinegars are more expensive in many cases, but they add so much amazing flavor for so few calories!

½ **cup champagne vinegar**

¼ **cup Dijon mustard**

1 teaspoon stevia honey blend sweetener (such as Truvia Nectar)

¼ **cup extra virgin olive oil**

1 Add the vinegar, mustard, and sweetener to a small mixing bowl. Using a small whisk, slowly whisk in the oil until it is emulsified (well combined). Use immediately or refrigerate it in an airtight container or salad cruet for up to 2 months.

CHOICES/EXCHANGES
1 fat

PER SERVING
40 calories, 3.5 g fat, 0.5 g saturated fat, 0 g trans fat, 0 mg cholesterol, 90 mg sodium, 5 mg potassium, 2 g carbohydrate, 0 g fiber, 0 g sugars, 0 g protein, 5 mg phosphorus

Devinly Warm Bacon Dressing

Warm bacon dressing? YES! I'm all about figuring out ways to allow you (and me—my interest in cooking did all start as a means to lose weight myself) to eat the foods you LOVE! That being said, this is one dressing you'll want to use sparingly. A little goes a long way. I consider this a "special occasion dressing," not one you use on everything all the time. But it's a great way to curb that bacon craving every once in a while!

½ cup lower sodium chicken broth

1 tablespoon apple cider vinegar

¼ teaspoon xanthan gum

½ tablespoon Dijon mustard

1 teaspoon stevia honey blend sweetener (such as Truvia Nectar)

3 slices (2 ½ ounces) center cut bacon (preferably nitrate free), finely chopped

3 tablespoons very finely chopped shallots

1 clove garlic, peeled and very finely chopped

Freshly ground black pepper, to taste

1 In a medium deep bowl, whisk together the broth, vinegar, and xanthan gum.

2 In a small mixing bowl, whisk together the mustard and sweetener until well combined. Slowly whisk in the broth mixture.

3 Place a small nonstick soup pot over medium high heat. Add the bacon and cook it, stirring frequently, until completely crisp (obviously not burnt, but it should be very crispy), about 4–6 minutes. Drain the bacon from the bacon grease, reserving the grease, and set the bacon aside.

4 Add 1 tablespoon of bacon grease back into the pot and place it over medium heat. Add the shallots and garlic. Cook them until fragrant, about 30 seconds. Whisk in the mustard mixture and reduce it, stirring frequently, until it is thickened slightly to the consistency of a gravy, 1–2 minutes.

5 Remove the dressing from the pan (it will continue to thicken slightly). Season it with pepper. Enjoy immediately or refrigerate it in an airtight container, then reheat it before enjoying. The reserved bacon should be added back into the dressing just before serving.

CHOICES/EXCHANGES
½ fat

PER SERVING
30 calories, 2 g fat, 0.8 g saturated fat, 0 g trans fat, 2 mg cholesterol, 90 mg sodium, 35 mg potassium, 1 g carbohydrate, 0 g fiber, 0 g sugars, 1 g protein, 15 mg phosphorus

Body Lovin' Bruschetta

1 ⅓ cups finely chopped, seeded Roma (plum) tomatoes

1 tablespoon thinly slivered fresh basil leaves (aka basil chiffonade)

1 tablespoon extra virgin olive oil

½ tablespoon balsamic vinegar

¼ teaspoon salt

1 ½ teaspoons freshly minced garlic

1/16 teaspoon freshly ground black pepper, or to taste

1 Mix the tomatoes, basil, olive oil, vinegar, salt, garlic, and pepper in a medium resealable container. Cover with the lid and refrigerate the bruschetta for at least 2 hours for the flavors to meld. Serve cold or at room temperature. Enjoy!

Cook's Notes

I find that not many people know how to chiffonade basil, but it's so easy! I'm happy to show you how to create those perfect fine basil slivers that can add so much elegance to your dishes. Just visit me at **www.devinalexander.com/diabetes** and I'll show you via video.

CHOICES/EXCHANGES
½ fat

PER SERVING
20 calories, 2 g fat, 0.2 g saturated fat, 0 g trans fat, 0 mg cholesterol, 75 mg sodium, 75 mg potassium, 2 g carbohydrate, 0 g fiber, 1 g sugars, 0 g protein, 10 mg phosphorus

Peanut Satay Sauce

You may want to consider doubling the recipe for this addictive sauce. I'm a single person so one serving is totally enough for me with some left over for later enjoyment. But if you're a family of four who wants to make my Thai Shrimp Flatbread Pizza (see page 41) or you're entertaining, then it definitely makes sense to consider doubling or even tripling this recipe. It doubles easily and the cooking times stay the same, so have no fear!

Olive oil spray (propellant free)

1 tablespoon freshly minced garlic

1 tablespoon finely chopped whole green onion

3 tablespoons light coconut milk

¼ cup low sodium chicken broth or low sodium vegetable broth

1 teaspoon brown sugar

1 tablespoon lower sodium soy sauce

1 tablespoon lime juice

1 teaspoon very finely chopped peeled ginger

¼ teaspoon sriracha (preferably natural)

¼ cup natural, smooth peanut butter

1 Lightly mist a small nonstick soup pot with spray and place it over medium heat. Add the garlic and green onion and cook them, stirring occasionally, until they begin to soften and become very fragrant, about 2 minutes.

2 Add the coconut milk, broth, brown sugar, soy sauce, lime juice, ginger, and sriracha. Using a whisk for ease, stir them until well combined. Bring the mixture to a simmer. Simmer it, stirring frequently, for just 5 minutes—the simmer melds the flavors and softens the veggies. Be careful not to overboil the mixture; you don't want the liquid to reduce.

3 After 5 minutes, remove the pot from the heat. Slowly whisk in the peanut butter until it is well incorporated. Immediately transfer the sauce to a serving bowl (if you leave it in the pot, the residual heat could over thicken it). Enjoy immediately.

Cook's Notes

Use the light coconut milk that you find in the international aisle in your local grocery store.

If I'm making this sauce for non-vegetarians, I always use chicken broth because my local grocery stores don't carry a veggie broth that is as low in sodium as low sodium chicken broth. If you decide to use veggie broth, look for the lowest sodium variety available.

Look for a natural peanut butter with only peanuts and salt in the ingredient list.

This recipe should yield ¾ cup of sauce. If it doesn't, add additional broth to thin it out so you don't overconsume a concentration of the ingredients.

CHOICES/EXCHANGES
1 ½ fat

PER SERVING
80 calories, 6 g fat, 1.1 g saturated fat, 0 g trans fat, 0 mg cholesterol, 140 mg sodium, 115 mg potassium, 4 g carbohydrate, 1 g fiber, 1 g sugars, 4 g protein, 55 mg phosphorus

ROASTED RED PEPPERS • 196

The Basics

DONE RIGHT

Have-On-Hand Grilled Chicken

This chicken is perfect to keep on hand for munching or for using in dishes like salads, sandwiches, quesadillas, and more. If you buy your chicken in bulk and cook extra, you'll save time and money when hunger and the dinner hour strike. After all, ask any trainer or health professional: having options at your fingertips is the best way to ensure you won't get "stuck" eating something not-so-clean for convenience.

Don't know how or why to pound a chicken breast? Don't know how to make sure you're not overcooking your chicken? Visit me at www.devinalexander.com/diabetes and I'll show you how to properly cook chicken. Plus I'll reveal a ton of chef secrets to make your kitchen more practical and your dishes more Devinly decadent!

4 (4 ounce) trimmed, boneless, skinless chicken breasts (preferably free range), pounded to ½ inch thickness

1 teaspoon extra virgin olive oil

⅛ teaspoon sea salt

Freshly ground black pepper, to taste

1 Preheat a grill to high.

2 Add the chicken breasts to a medium bowl. Drizzle the oil over them and then sprinkle with the salt and pepper. Toss them until they are evenly coated.

3 Place the chicken breasts side by side on the grill, smooth sides down. Turn the heat to medium, if possible, or place them away from direct heat if you don't have temperature control. Grill them until the chicken is no longer pink and the juices run clear, about 3–5 minutes per side.

4 Remove from the grill and tent the chicken breasts with foil. Let them rest for 3 minutes before cutting them. Enjoy immediately or cool them and store them in an airtight container in the refrigerator for up to 3 days.

CHOICES/EXCHANGES
3 lean protein

PER SERVING
140 calories, 4 g fat, 0.9 g saturated fat, 0 g trans fat, 65 mg cholesterol, 125 mg sodium, 190 mg potassium, 0 g carbohydrate, 0 g fiber, 0 g sugars, 24 g protein, 175 mg phosphorus

Quinoa Cooking Instructions

I've been eating quinoa for decades. When I first found it, I tried to include it in cooking demos and people kept saying that they wouldn't eat it because it "looked like bird seed". Now it's mainstream and I couldn't be happier.

Many packages recommend you cook your quinoa with a lot more water than I use in this recipe. Perhaps it's because I'm Italian and I grew up eating pasta, but I like my quinoa a little "al dente". I'm just not a fan of (what I consider) mushy pasta, quinoa, or any grain for that matter. But if you prefer a really soft quinoa, go for it. Adding extra water never hurt anyone, and your dish may even yield greater volume than my recipe. Just be careful—if you think your quinoa tastes bitter, it might be because of that extra water in conjunction with the longer cooking time!

1 cup quinoa

1 cup water

1 Place the quinoa in a fine sieve and rinse it until the water runs clear. Shake off any excess water. Then transfer the quinoa to a small soup pot with a lid. Add the water. Turn the heat to high. When the water comes to a boil, cover the pot and reduce the heat so the quinoa simmers. Simmer for 20 minutes or until all of the water is absorbed.

2 Turn off the heat and let the quinoa rest, covered, for 5 minutes. Fluff the quinoa and serve.

CHOICES/EXCHANGES

1 starch

PER SERVING

100 calories, 1.5 g fat, 0.2 g saturated fat, 0 g trans fat, 0 mg cholesterol, 0 mg sodium, 150 mg potassium, 17 g carbohydrate, 2 g fiber, 0 g sugars, 4 g protein, 120 mg phosphorus

Farro Cooking Instructions

If you're not familiar with it, farro is an ancient, unprocessed wheat grain that is high in fiber and has a nutty flavor. I love farro! It's become a hit on many gourmet restaurant menus in recent years and it frequents my kitchen too!

1 ½ cups water

1 cup dry farro

1 Add the water to a small soup pot along with the farro. Place the pot over high heat. When the water comes to a boil, lower the heat to bring the farro to a simmer.

2 Cover the pot and simmer the farro until all of the water is absorbed, about 25–30 minutes. Let it rest, covered, for 5 minutes.

CHOICES/EXCHANGES
1 ½ starch

PER SERVING
120 calories, 1 g fat, 0.1 g saturated fat, 0 g trans fat, 0 mg cholesterol, 0 mg sodium, 140 mg potassium, 26 g carbohydrate, 4 g fiber, 0 g sugars, 5 g protein, 145 mg phosphorus

Roasted Garlic

Roasted garlic adds so much flavor to a dish, which allows you to cut back on sodium and other not-so-good-for-you ingredients. If you've never tried baking garlic in bread or in pizza dough, you're missing out! When making this recipe, remember to use no more than ½ teaspoon of olive oil per head of garlic.

Head(s) of garlic

½ teaspoon extra virgin olive oil (per head of garlic)

1 Preheat the oven to 400°F.

2 Cut the tip off of each head of garlic to expose the tops of the cloves, leaving the root and cloves intact. Peel the outer pieces of the papery skin away (but not so much of it that the cloves separate from the head).

3 Sit each garlic head in a cup of a standard muffin tin (for ease), cut side up. Drizzle ½ teaspoon of olive oil over each head, rubbing it into the exposed part of the garlic cloves. Cover the top of each head with aluminum foil. Roast the head(s) until the cloves are very tender, about 35–45 minutes.

4 Remove the garlic from the oven and allow it to cool. When cool enough to handle, squeeze the roasted garlic from the skins, discarding all skins. Enjoy immediately, and store any leftover roasted garlic in an airtight container in the refrigerator for up to 3 days.

CHOICES/EXCHANGES
This recipe has less than 20 calories and 5 g or less of carbohydrate per serving.

PER SERVING
10 calories, 0 g fat, 0.1 g saturated fat, 0 g trans fat, 0 mg cholesterol, 0 mg sodium, 20 mg potassium, 2 g carbohydrate, 0 g fiber, 0 g sugars, 0 g protein, 10 mg phosphorus

Roasted Red Peppers

Making your own roasted red peppers is simple once you know the technique. All you need are red bell peppers and a heat source.

Small (about 5 ounce) red bell pepper(s)

1 Preheat a broiler or grill to high heat. Using a knife, poke a couple of holes in the top of the bell pepper(s) so they don't explode. Place the pepper(s) on the top rack of the oven (place a piece of foil or a baking sheet on the rack underneath them in case the peppers drip) or place directly on the grill.

2 As soon as the pepper skins turn black, after about 2–5 minutes, rotate the pepper(s) so that another side faces the heat. If you continue cooking them on the same side after the skins are blackened, you'll start to burn the pepper itself. Continue until the skins on all four sides are charred and black (if you've never roasted your own peppers before, be aware that they will look burnt when you remove them from the oven/grill).

3 Place the pepper(s) in a brown paper bag and close the bag (place it in a bowl or on a baking tray to avoid a mess). Let the pepper(s) rest until no longer too hot to touch, approximately 15 minutes. Remove the pepper(s) from the paper bag and peel away the charred skins—they should easily peel from the flesh of the pepper(s). Discard the skin, and remove the core and seeds.

CHOICES/EXCHANGES
1 nonstarchy vegetable

PER SERVING
25 calories, 0 g fat, 0 g saturated fat, 0 g trans fat, 0 mg cholesterol, 0 mg sodium, 160 mg potassium, 6 g carbohydrate, 1 g fiber, 4 g sugars, 1 g protein, 15 mg phosphorus

Index

*Note: Page numbers in **bold** refer to photographs.*